L'ART DE VIVRE!

the of living

VISUALIZE A DAY IN YOUR DREAM LIFE AND WRITE IT HERE.
DREAM BIG. MONEY IS NO OBJECT.

who would be with you? how do you FEEL?

what do you see? what do you hear?

be SPECIFIC!

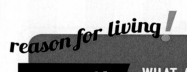

RAISON D'ÊTRE!

WHAT ARE YOUR TOP 2-3 PRIORITIES (FAMILY, HEALTH, CAREER, FAITH ETC)?
WRITE HERE. WHEN MAKING DECISIONS ASK YOURSELF
"does this honor my top priorities?" IF NOT . . . ..POLITELY DECLINE.

PAIN AU CHOCOLAT

FOR YOUR BRAIN!

WRITE YOUR TOP MANTRAS AND AFFIRMATIONS HERE!
"every day and every way i'm getting better and better. i am happy, i am healthy."

EX

" *life is beautiful* "

GRATITUDE. BRAIN DUMP EVERYTHING YOU ARE GRATEFUL FOR

be SPECIFIC!

VIVRE LA VIE PAR LA CONCEPTION!

living a life by design. create your joyful life!

WRITE YOUR 10 GOALS FOR THE NEXT 1 YEAR HERE.
WHAT WILL BRING YOU JOY ??

1 --

2 --

3 --

4 --

5 --

6 --

7 --

8 --

9 --

10 --

I AM BRILLIANT
gorgeous
TALENTED AND FABULOUS

GOOD MORNING *gorgeous!*

I AM GRATEFUL FOR

_____

_____

_____

MY MANTRA *for today!*

_____

_____

_____

FUN!!! TODAY FOR FUN I WILL

_____

_____

_____

- [ ] VISUALIZATION – SET YOUR TIMER FOR A MINIMUM OF 5 MINUTES AND GO THERE!
- [ ] MEDITATION – SET YOUR TIMER FOR A MINIMUM OF 5 MINUTES AND BE PRESENT, IN THE NOW. BREATHE.
- [ ] EXERCISE – DID YOU MOVE AT LEAST 30 MINUTES TODAY?
- [ ] FUEL – EAT 80% NUTRIENT DENSE FOOD THAT ENERGIZES YOU

I WAS MOST GRATEFUL FOR TODAY

_____

_____

_____

_____

_____

_____

Good Evening Gorgeous!

I LOVE TO GIVE. TODAY I GAVE

_____

_____

_____

CHEERS TO ME!!!
LET'S CELEBRATE MY SUCCESSES FOR THE DAY

_____

_____

_____

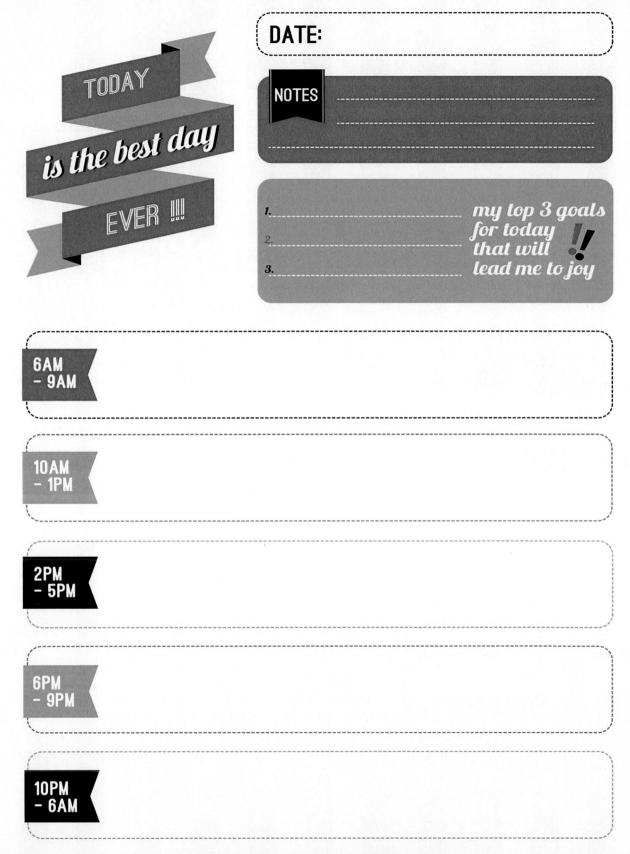

TODAY is the best day EVER !!!

DATE:

NOTES

1.
2.
3.

my top 3 goals
for today
that will
lead me to joy

6AM – 9AM

10AM – 1PM

2PM – 5PM

6PM – 9PM

10PM – 6AM

*make sure you get your sleep!

I AM BRILLIANT
gorgeous
TALENTED AND FABULOUS

GOOD MORNING *gorgeous!*

I AM GRATEFUL FOR

MY MANTRA

for today!

FUN!!! TODAY FOR FUN I WILL

☐ VISUALIZATION – SET YOUR TIMER FOR A MINIMUM OF 5 MINUTES AND GO THERE!

☐ MEDITATION – SET YOUR TIMER FOR A MINIMUM OF 5 MINUTES AND BE PRESENT, IN THE NOW. BREATHE.

☐ EXERCISE – DID YOU MOVE AT LEAST 30 MINUTES TODAY?

☐ FUEL – EAT 80% NUTRIENT DENSE FOOD THAT ENERGIZES YOU

I WAS MOST GRATEFUL FOR TODAY

Good Evening Gorgeous!

I LOVE TO GIVE.
TODAY I GAVE

CHEERS TO ME!!!
LET'S CELEBRATE MY SUCCESSES FOR THE DAY

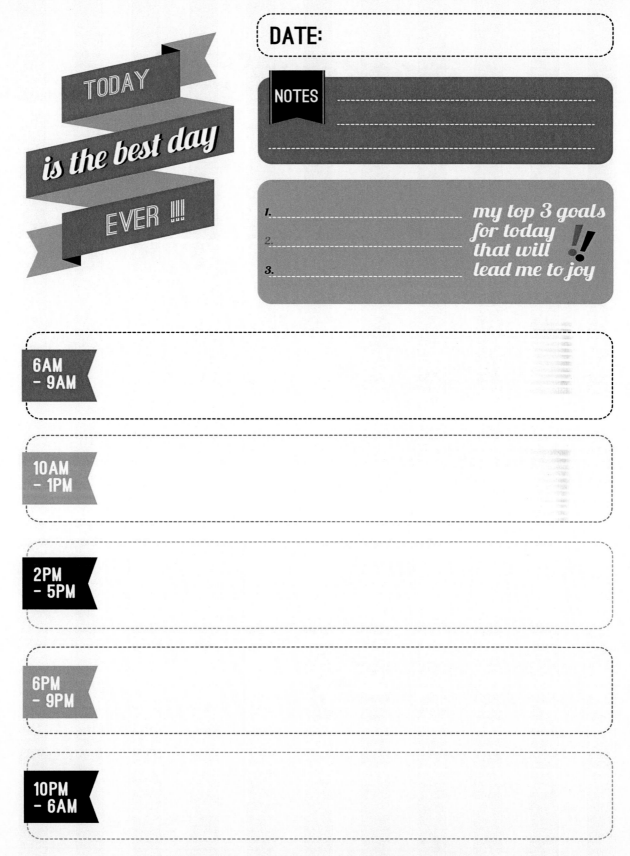

TODAY

is the best day

EVER !!!!

DATE:

NOTES

1.
2.
3.

my top 3 goals
for today
that will
lead me to joy

6AM
– 9AM

10AM
– 1PM

2PM
– 5PM

6PM
– 9PM

10PM
– 6AM

*make sure you get your sleep!

I AM BRILLIANT
gorgeous
TALENTED AND FABULOUS

GOOD MORNING
gorgeous!

I AM GRATEFUL FOR

MY
MANTRA

*for
today!*

FUN!!! TODAY FOR FUN I WILL

☐ VISUALIZATION – SET YOUR TIMER FOR A MINIMUM OF 5 MINUTES AND GO THERE!

☐ MEDITATION – SET YOUR TIMER FOR A MINIMUM OF 5 MINUTES AND BE PRESENT, IN THE NOW. BREATHE.

☐ EXERCISE – DID YOU MOVE AT LEAST 30 MINUTES TODAY?

☐ FUEL – EAT 80% NUTRIENT DENSE FOOD THAT ENERGIZES YOU

I WAS MOST GRATEFUL FOR TODAY

Good Evening Gorgeous!

I LOVE TO GIVE.
TODAY I GAVE

CHEERS TO ME!!!
LET'S CELEBRATE MY SUCCESSES FOR THE DAY

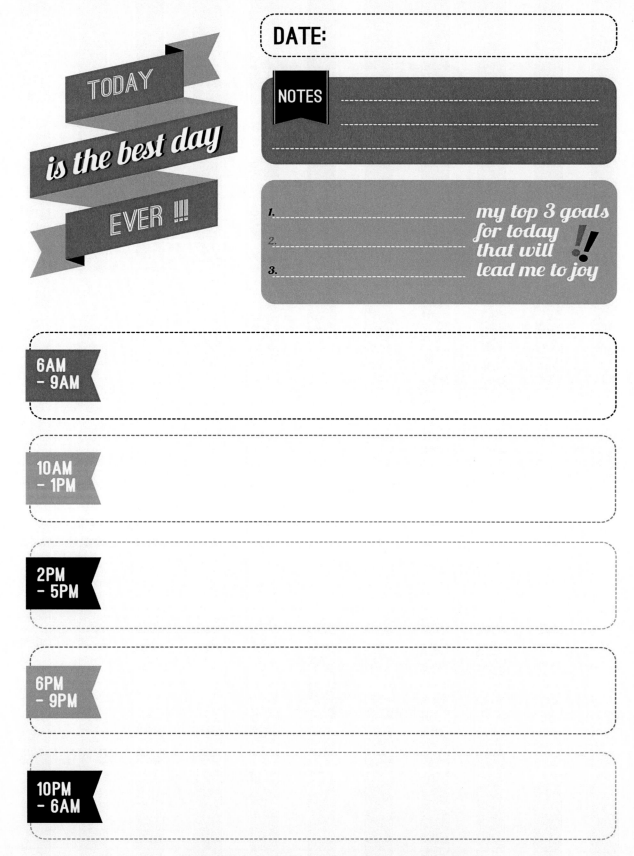

TODAY

is the best day

EVER !!!

DATE:

NOTES

1.

my top 3 goals

2.

for today that will

3.

lead me to joy

6AM – 9AM

10AM – 1PM

2PM – 5PM

6PM – 9PM

10PM – 6AM

make sure you get your sleep!

I AM BRILLIANT
gorgeous
TALENTED AND FABULOUS

GOOD MORNING *gorgeous!*

I AM GRATEFUL FOR

MY MANTRA

for today!

FUN!!! TODAY FOR FUN I WILL

☐ VISUALIZATION – SET YOUR TIMER FOR A MINIMUM OF 5 MINUTES AND GO THERE!

☐ MEDITATION – SET YOUR TIMER FOR A MINIMUM OF 5 MINUTES AND BE PRESENT, IN THE NOW. BREATHE.

☐ EXERCISE – DID YOU MOVE AT LEAST 30 MINUTES TODAY?

☐ FUEL – EAT 80% NUTRIENT DENSE FOOD THAT ENERGIZES YOU

I WAS MOST GRATEFUL FOR TODAY

Good Evening Gorgeous!

I LOVE TO GIVE. TODAY I GAVE

CHEERS TO ME!!!
LET'S CELEBRATE MY SUCCESSES FOR THE DAY

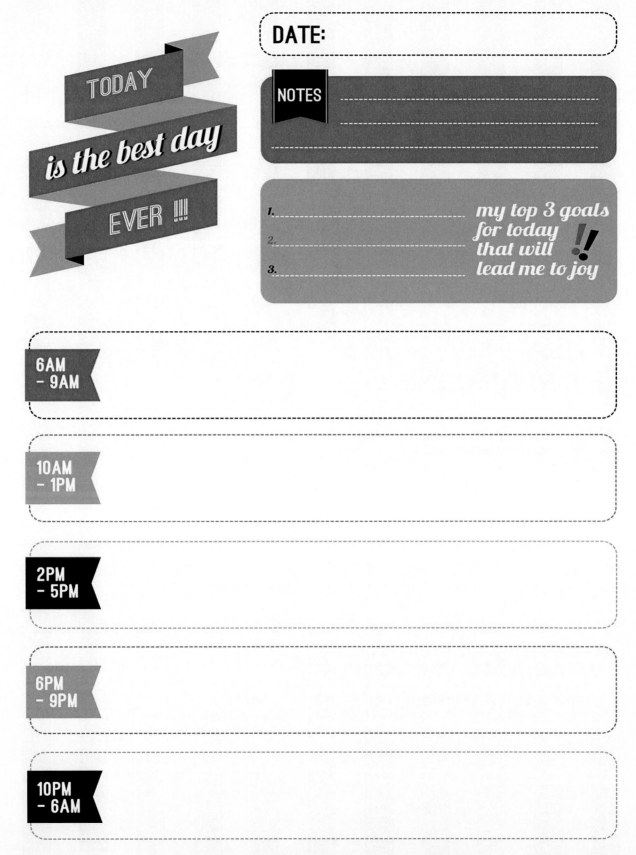

TODAY

is the best day

EVER !!!

DATE:

NOTES

1.
2.
3.

*my top 3 goals
for today
that will
lead me to joy*

6AM – 9AM

10AM – 1PM

2PM – 5PM

6PM – 9PM

10PM – 6AM

make sure you get your sleep!

I AM BRILLIANT
gorgeous
TALENTED AND FABULOUS

GOOD MORNING *gorgeous!*

I AM GRATEFUL FOR

MY MANTRA

for today!

FUN!!! TODAY FOR FUN I WILL

☐ VISUALIZATION – SET YOUR TIMER FOR A MINIMUM OF 5 MINUTES AND GO THERE!

☐ MEDITATION – SET YOUR TIMER FOR A MINIMUM OF 5 MINUTES AND BE PRESENT, IN THE NOW. BREATHE.

☐ EXERCISE – DID YOU MOVE AT LEAST 30 MINUTES TODAY?

☐ FUEL – EAT 80% NUTRIENT DENSE FOOD THAT ENERGIZES YOU

I WAS MOST GRATEFUL FOR TODAY

Good Evening Gorgeous!

I LOVE TO GIVE. TODAY I GAVE

CHEERS TO ME!!!
LET'S CELEBRATE MY SUCCESSES FOR THE DAY

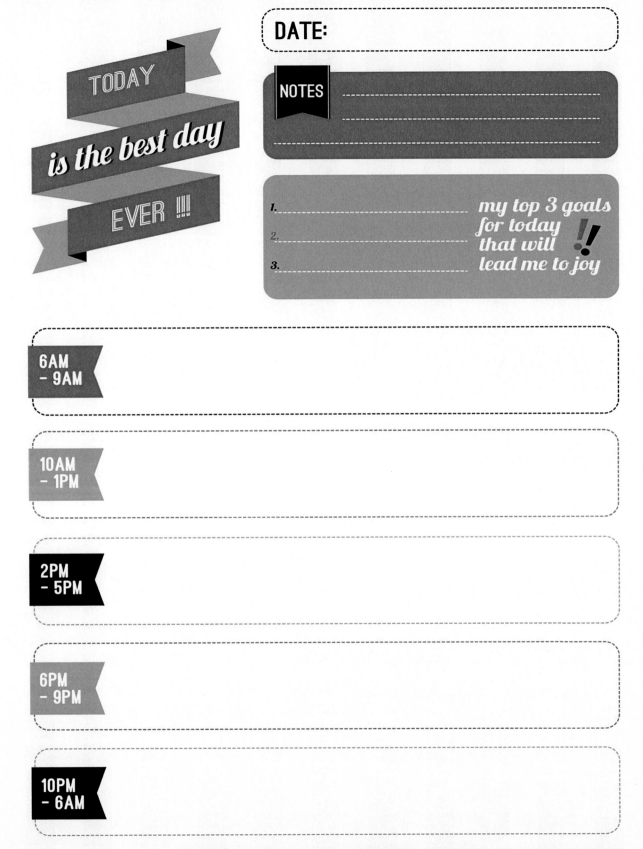

TODAY

is the best day

EVER !!!

DATE:

NOTES

1.
2.
3.

*my top 3 goals
for today
that will !!
lead me to joy*

6AM
- 9AM

10AM
- 1PM

2PM
- 5PM

6PM
- 9PM

10PM
- 6AM

make sure you get your sleep!

I AM BRILLIANT
gorgeous
TALENTED AND FABULOUS

GOOD MORNING *gorgeous!*

I AM GRATEFUL FOR

MY MANTRA

for today!

FUN!!! TODAY FOR FUN I WILL

- ☐ VISUALIZATION – SET YOUR TIMER FOR A MINIMUM OF 5 MINUTES AND GO THERE!
- ☐ MEDITATION – SET YOUR TIMER FOR A MINIMUM OF 5 MINUTES AND BE PRESENT, IN THE NOW. BREATHE.
- ☐ EXERCISE – DID YOU MOVE AT LEAST 30 MINUTES TODAY?
- ☐ FUEL – EAT 80% NUTRIENT DENSE FOOD THAT ENERGIZES YOU

I WAS MOST GRATEFUL FOR TODAY

Good Evening Gorgeous!

I LOVE TO GIVE.
TODAY I GAVE

CHEERS TO ME!!!
LET'S CELEBRATE MY SUCCESSES FOR THE DAY

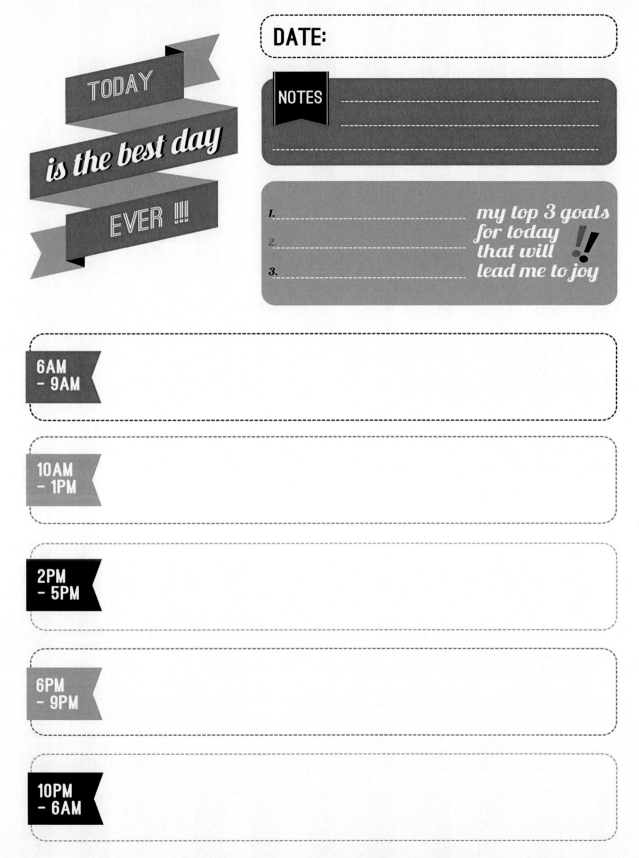

TODAY
is the best day
EVER !!!

DATE:

NOTES

1.
2.
3.

my top 3 goals
for today
that will
lead me to joy

6AM – 9AM

10AM – 1PM

2PM – 5PM

6PM – 9PM

10PM – 6AM

*make sure you get your sleep!

I AM BRILLIANT
gorgeous
TALENTED AND FABULOUS

GOOD MORNING
gorgeous!

I AM GRATEFUL FOR

MY MANTRA

for today!

FUN!!! TODAY FOR FUN I WILL

- [ ] VISUALIZATION – SET YOUR TIMER FOR A MINIMUM OF 5 MINUTES AND GO THERE!
- [ ] MEDITATION – SET YOUR TIMER FOR A MINIMUM OF 5 MINUTES AND BE PRESENT, IN THE NOW. BREATHE.
- [ ] EXERCISE – DID YOU MOVE AT LEAST 30 MINUTES TODAY?
- [ ] FUEL – EAT 80% NUTRIENT DENSE FOOD THAT ENERGIZES YOU

I WAS MOST GRATEFUL FOR TODAY

Good Evening Gorgeous!

I LOVE TO GIVE.
TODAY I GAVE

CHEERS TO ME!!!
LET'S CELEBRATE MY SUCCESSES FOR THE DAY

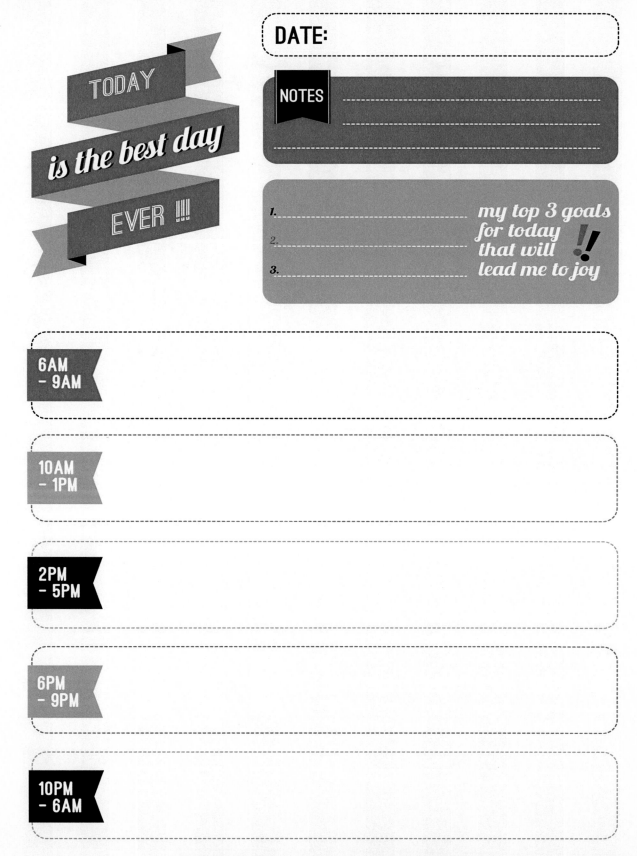

TODAY
is the best day
EVER !!!

DATE:

NOTES

1.
2.
3.
my top 3 goals
for today
that will
lead me to joy

6AM
- 9AM

10AM
- 1PM

2PM
- 5PM

6PM
- 9PM

10PM
- 6AM

*make sure you get your sleep!

I AM BRILLIANT
gorgeous
TALENTED AND FABULOUS

GOOD MORNING
gorgeous!

I AM GRATEFUL FOR

MY MANTRA

for today!

FUN!!! TODAY FOR FUN I WILL

☐ VISUALIZATION – SET YOUR TIMER FOR A MINIMUM OF 5 MINUTES AND GO THERE!

☐ MEDITATION – SET YOUR TIMER FOR A MINIMUM OF 5 MINUTES AND BE PRESENT, IN THE NOW. BREATHE.

☐ EXERCISE – DID YOU MOVE AT LEAST 30 MINUTES TODAY?

☐ FUEL – EAT 80% NUTRIENT DENSE FOOD THAT ENERGIZES YOU

I WAS MOST GRATEFUL FOR TODAY

Good Evening Gorgeous!

I LOVE TO GIVE.
TODAY I GAVE

CHEERS TO ME!!!
LET'S CELEBRATE MY SUCCESSES FOR THE DAY

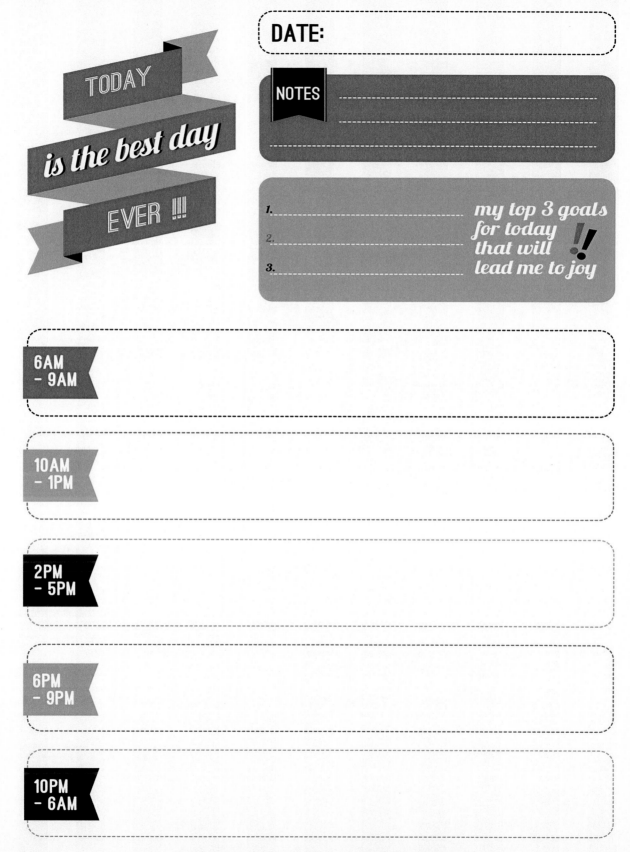

TODAY

is the best day

EVER !!!

DATE:

NOTES

1. ....
2. ....
3. ....

my top 3 goals
for today
that will
lead me to joy

6AM
– 9AM

10AM
– 1PM

2PM
– 5PM

6PM
– 9PM

10PM
– 6AM

*make sure you get your sleep!

I AM BRILLIANT
gorgeous
TALENTED AND FABULOUS

GOOD MORNING *gorgeous!*

I AM GRATEFUL FOR

MY MANTRA

for today!

FUN!!! TODAY FOR FUN I WILL

☐ VISUALIZATION - SET YOUR TIMER FOR A MINIMUM OF 5 MINUTES AND GO THERE!

☐ MEDITATION - SET YOUR TIMER FOR A MINIMUM OF 5 MINUTES AND BE PRESENT, IN THE NOW. BREATHE.

☐ EXERCISE - DID YOU MOVE AT LEAST 30 MINUTES TODAY?

☐ FUEL - EAT 80% NUTRIENT DENSE FOOD THAT ENERGIZES YOU

I WAS MOST GRATEFUL FOR TODAY

Good Evening Gorgeous!

I LOVE TO GIVE. TODAY I GAVE

CHEERS TO ME!!!
LET'S CELEBRATE MY SUCCESSES FOR THE DAY

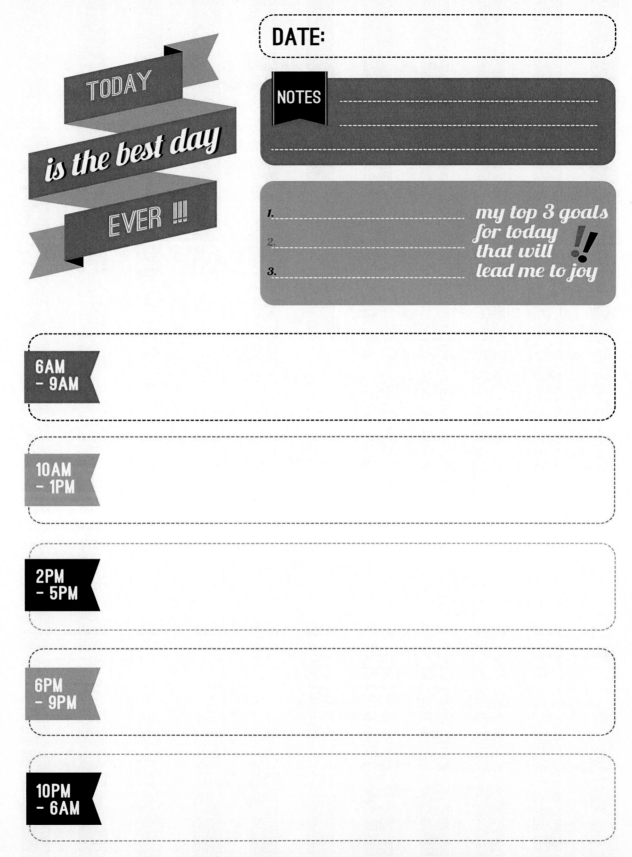

TODAY

is the best day

EVER !!!

DATE:

NOTES ----------------------------------

----

1. ----------------------------------
2. ----------------------------------
3. ----------------------------------

my top 3 goals for today that will **!!** *lead me to joy*

6AM – 9AM

10AM – 1PM

2PM – 5PM

6PM – 9PM

10PM – 6AM

make sure you get your sleep!

I AM BRILLIANT
gorgeous
TALENTED AND FABULOUS

GOOD MORNING
gorgeous!

I AM GRATEFUL FOR

MY MANTRA

for today!

FUN!!! TODAY FOR FUN I WILL

☐ VISUALIZATION – SET YOUR TIMER FOR A MINIMUM OF 5 MINUTES AND GO THERE!

☐ MEDITATION – SET YOUR TIMER FOR A MINIMUM OF 5 MINUTES AND BE PRESENT, IN THE NOW. BREATHE.

☐ EXERCISE – DID YOU MOVE AT LEAST 30 MINUTES TODAY?

☐ FUEL – EAT 80% NUTRIENT DENSE FOOD THAT ENERGIZES YOU

I WAS MOST GRATEFUL FOR TODAY

Good Evening Gorgeous!

I LOVE TO GIVE.
TODAY I GAVE

CHEERS TO ME!!!
LET'S CELEBRATE MY SUCCESSES FOR THE DAY

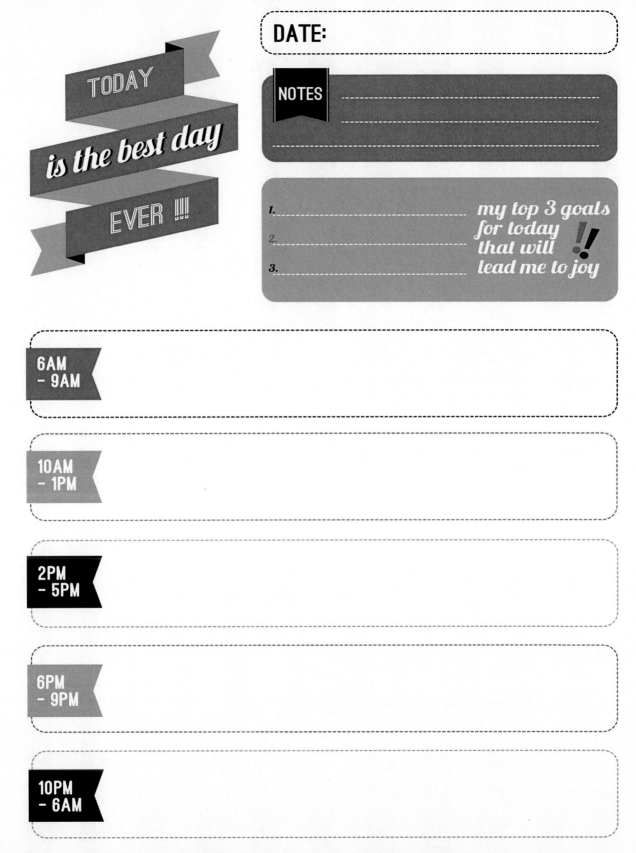

TODAY
is the best day
EVER !!!

DATE:

NOTES

1.
2.
3.

my top 3 goals for today that will lead me to joy !!

6AM – 9AM

10AM – 1PM

2PM – 5PM

6PM – 9PM

10PM – 6AM

make sure you get your sleep!

I AM BRILLIANT
gorgeous
TALENTED AND FABULOUS

GOOD MORNING *gorgeous!*

I AM GRATEFUL FOR

MY MANTRA

for today!

FUN!!! TODAY FOR FUN I WILL

- ☐ **VISUALIZATION** – SET YOUR TIMER FOR A MINIMUM OF 5 MINUTES AND GO THERE!
- ☐ **MEDITATION** – SET YOUR TIMER FOR A MINIMUM OF 5 MINUTES AND BE PRESENT, IN THE NOW. BREATHE.
- ☐ **EXERCISE** – DID YOU MOVE AT LEAST 30 MINUTES TODAY?
- ☐ **FUEL** – EAT 80% NUTRIENT DENSE FOOD THAT ENERGIZES YOU

I WAS MOST GRATEFUL FOR TODAY

Good Evening Gorgeous!

I LOVE TO GIVE. TODAY I GAVE

CHEERS TO ME!!!
LET'S CELEBRATE MY SUCCESSES FOR THE DAY

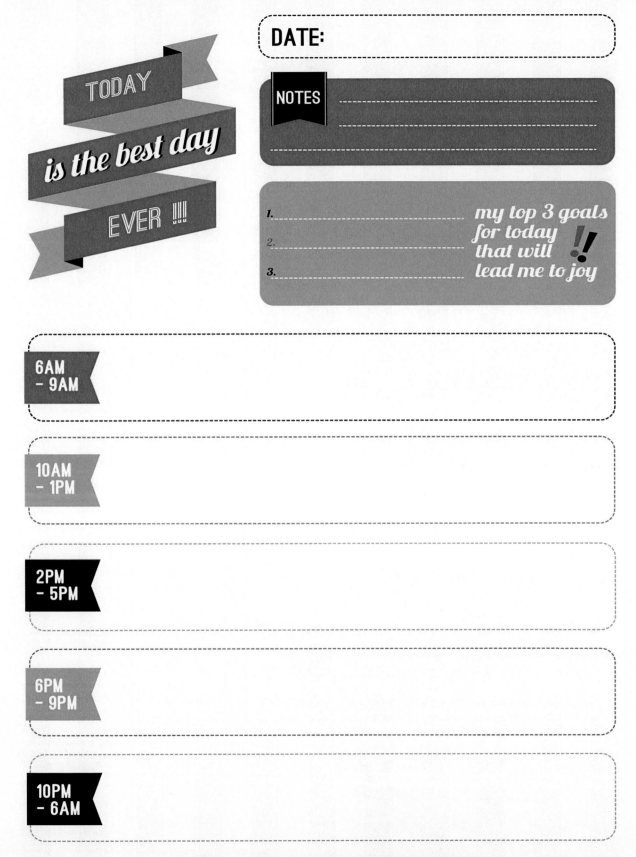

TODAY

is the best day

EVER !!!

DATE:

NOTES

1.
2.
3.
my top 3 goals
for today
that will
lead me to joy

6AM
– 9AM

10AM
– 1PM

2PM
– 5PM

6PM
– 9PM

10PM
– 6AM

*make sure you get your sleep!

I AM BRILLIANT
gorgeous
TALENTED AND FABULOUS

GOOD MORNING *gorgeous!*

I AM GRATEFUL FOR

MY MANTRA

for today!

FUN!!! TODAY FOR FUN I WILL

☐ VISUALIZATION – SET YOUR TIMER FOR A MINIMUM OF 5 MINUTES AND GO THERE!

☐ MEDITATION – SET YOUR TIMER FOR A MINIMUM OF 5 MINUTES AND BE PRESENT, IN THE NOW. BREATHE.

☐ EXERCISE – DID YOU MOVE AT LEAST 30 MINUTES TODAY?

☐ FUEL – EAT 80% NUTRIENT DENSE FOOD THAT ENERGIZES YOU

I WAS MOST GRATEFUL FOR TODAY

Good Evening Gorgeous!

I LOVE TO GIVE. TODAY I GAVE

CHEERS TO ME!!!
LET'S CELEBRATE MY SUCCESSES FOR THE DAY

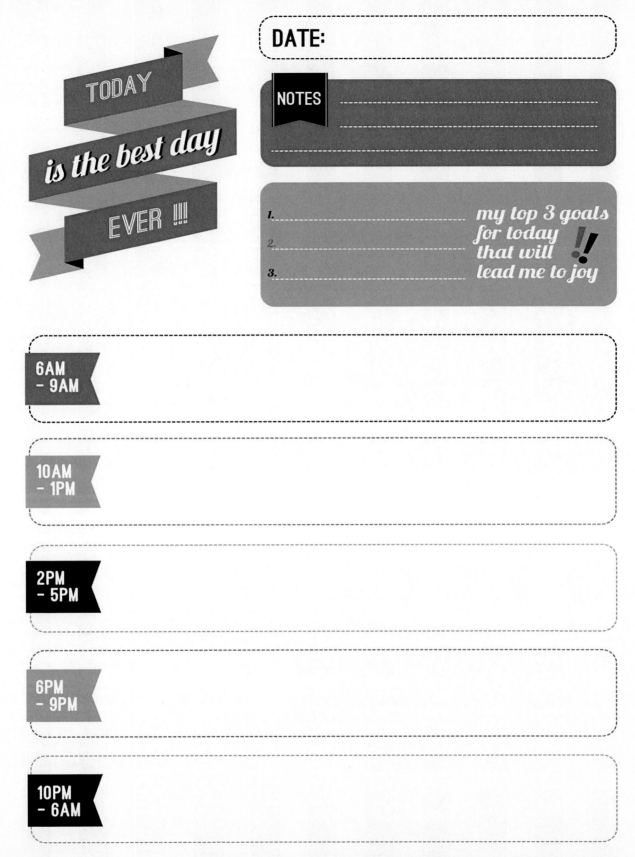

TODAY is the best day EVER !!!

DATE:

NOTES

1.
2.
3.

my top 3 goals for today that will lead me to joy

6AM – 9AM

10AM – 1PM

2PM – 5PM

6PM – 9PM

10PM – 6AM

*make sure you get your sleep!

I AM BRILLIANT
gorgeous
TALENTED AND FABULOUS

GOOD MORNING *gorgeous!*

I AM GRATEFUL FOR

MY MANTRA

for today!

FUN!!! TODAY FOR FUN I WILL

- ☐ VISUALIZATION – SET YOUR TIMER FOR A MINIMUM OF 5 MINUTES AND GO THERE!
- ☐ MEDITATION – SET YOUR TIMER FOR A MINIMUM OF 5 MINUTES AND BE PRESENT, IN THE NOW. BREATHE.
- ☐ EXERCISE – DID YOU MOVE AT LEAST 30 MINUTES TODAY?
- ☐ FUEL – EAT 80% NUTRIENT DENSE FOOD THAT ENERGIZES YOU

Good Evening Gorgeous!

I WAS MOST GRATEFUL FOR TODAY

I LOVE TO GIVE.
TODAY I GAVE

CHEERS TO ME!!!
LET'S CELEBRATE MY SUCCESSES FOR THE DAY

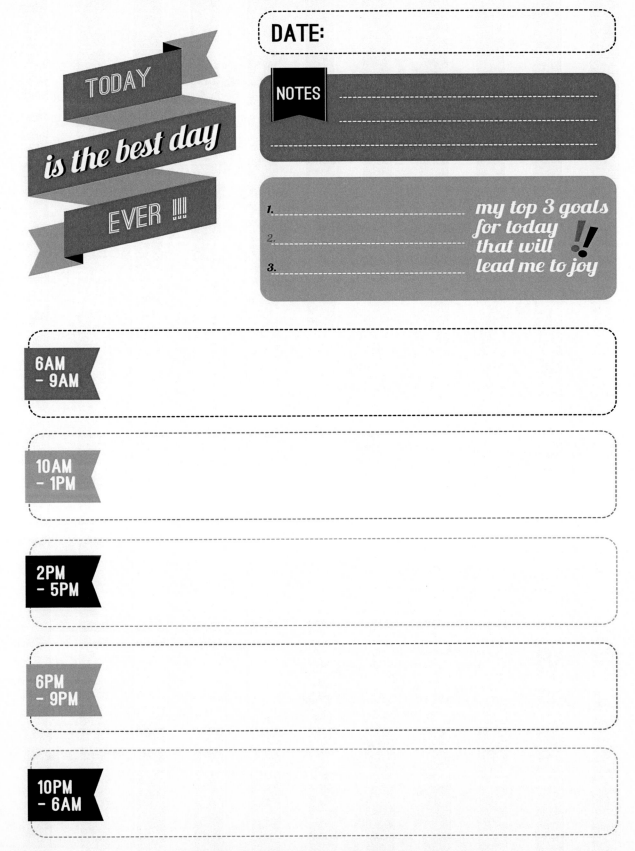

TODAY
is the best day
EVER !!!

DATE:

NOTES

1.
2.
3.
my top 3 goals
for today
that will
lead me to joy

6AM
– 9AM

10AM
– 1PM

2PM
– 5PM

6PM
– 9PM

10PM
– 6AM

make sure you get your sleep!

I AM BRILLIANT
gorgeous
TALENTED AND FABULOUS

GOOD MORNING *gorgeous!*

MY MANTRA

for today!

I AM GRATEFUL FOR

FUN!!! TODAY FOR FUN I WILL

- [ ] VISUALIZATION – SET YOUR TIMER FOR A MINIMUM OF 5 MINUTES AND GO THERE!
- [ ] MEDITATION – SET YOUR TIMER FOR A MINIMUM OF 5 MINUTES AND BE PRESENT, IN THE NOW. BREATHE.
- [ ] EXERCISE – DID YOU MOVE AT LEAST 30 MINUTES TODAY?
- [ ] FUEL – EAT 80% NUTRIENT DENSE FOOD THAT ENERGIZES YOU

I WAS MOST GRATEFUL FOR TODAY

Good Evening Gorgeous!

I LOVE TO GIVE.
TODAY I GAVE

CHEERS TO ME!!!
LET'S CELEBRATE MY SUCCESSES FOR THE DAY

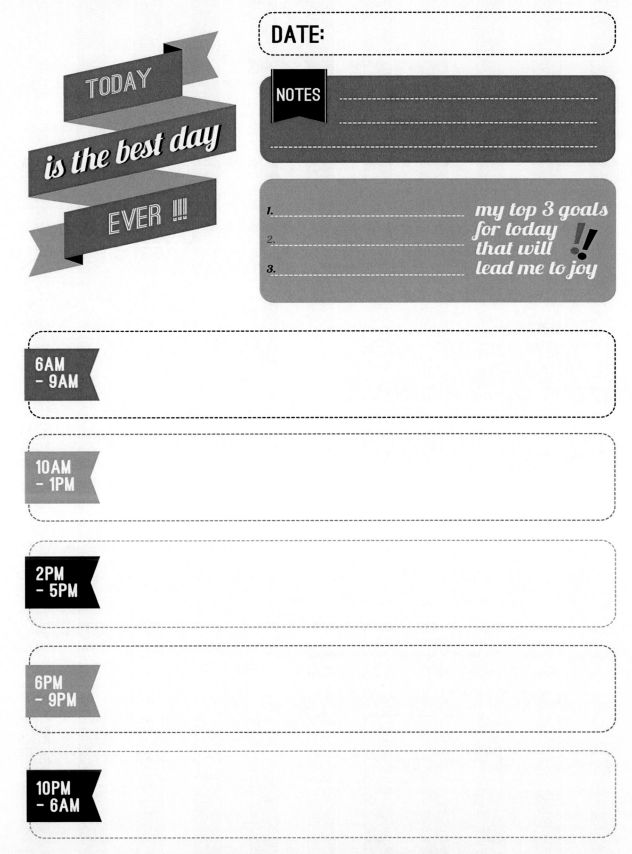

TODAY

is the best day

EVER !!!

DATE:

NOTES

1.
2.
3.

*my top 3 goals
for today
that will
lead me to joy*

6AM – 9AM

10AM – 1PM

2PM – 5PM

6PM – 9PM

10PM – 6AM

*make sure you get your sleep!

I AM BRILLIANT
gorgeous
TALENTED AND FABULOUS

GOOD MORNING *gorgeous!*

I AM GRATEFUL FOR

MY MANTRA

for today!

FUN!!! TODAY FOR FUN I WILL

- [ ] VISUALIZATION – SET YOUR TIMER FOR A MINIMUM OF 5 MINUTES AND GO THERE!
- [ ] MEDITATION – SET YOUR TIMER FOR A MINIMUM OF 5 MINUTES AND BE PRESENT, IN THE NOW. BREATHE.
- [ ] EXERCISE – DID YOU MOVE AT LEAST 30 MINUTES TODAY?
- [ ] FUEL – EAT 80% NUTRIENT DENSE FOOD THAT ENERGIZES YOU

I WAS MOST GRATEFUL FOR TODAY

Good Evening Gorgeous!

I LOVE TO GIVE. TODAY I GAVE

CHEERS TO ME!!!
LET'S CELEBRATE MY SUCCESSES FOR THE DAY

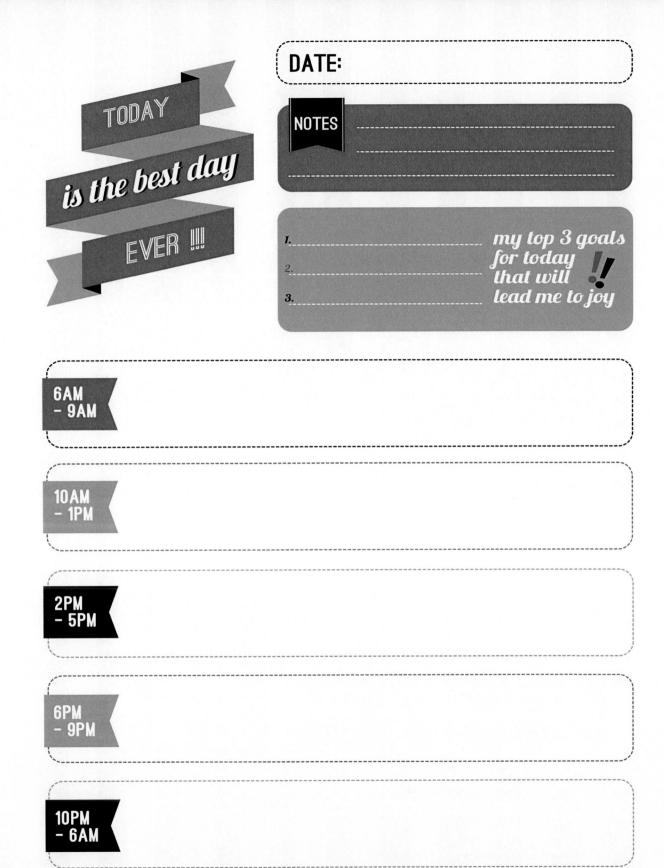

TODAY *is the best day* **EVER !!!**

DATE:

NOTES ....
....
....

1. ....
2. ....
3. ....

my top 3 goals for today that will lead me to joy !!

6AM – 9AM

10AM – 1PM

2PM – 5PM

6PM – 9PM

10PM – 6AM

make sure you get your sleep!

I AM BRILLIANT
gorgeous
TALENTED AND FABULOUS

GOOD MORNING *gorgeous!*

I AM GRATEFUL FOR

MY MANTRA

for today!

FUN!!! TODAY FOR FUN I WILL

- ☐ VISUALIZATION - SET YOUR TIMER FOR A MINIMUM OF 5 MINUTES AND GO THERE!
- ☐ MEDITATION - SET YOUR TIMER FOR A MINIMUM OF 5 MINUTES AND BE PRESENT, IN THE NOW. BREATHE.
- ☐ EXERCISE - DID YOU MOVE AT LEAST 30 MINUTES TODAY?
- ☐ FUEL - EAT 80% NUTRIENT DENSE FOOD THAT ENERGIZES YOU

I WAS MOST GRATEFUL FOR TODAY

Good Evening Gorgeous!

I LOVE TO GIVE. TODAY I GAVE

CHEERS TO ME!!!
LET'S CELEBRATE MY SUCCESSES FOR THE DAY

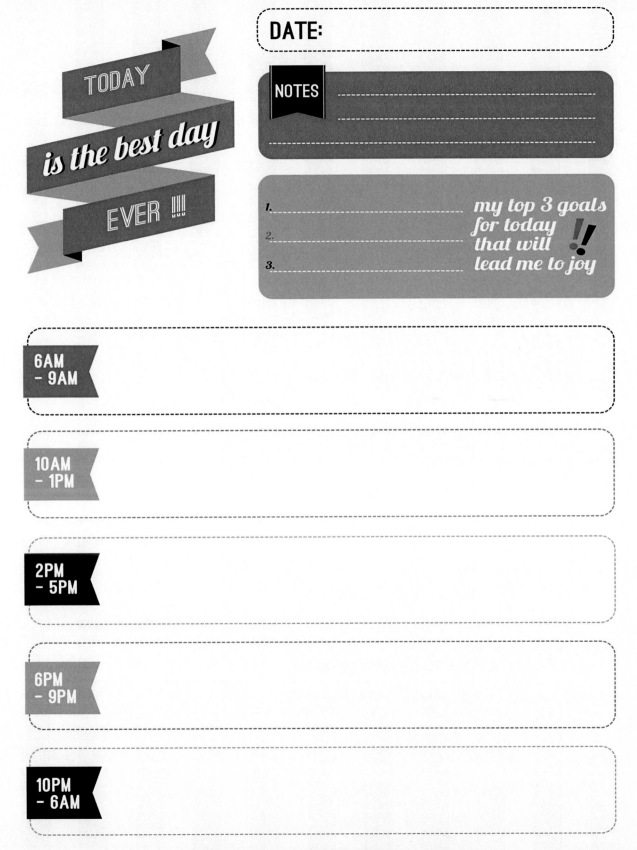

TODAY is the best day EVER !!!

DATE:

NOTES

----

1. -
2. -
3. -

my top 3 goals for today that will lead me to joy

6AM – 9AM

10AM – 1PM

2PM – 5PM

6PM – 9PM

10PM – 6AM

make sure you get your sleep!

I AM BRILLIANT
gorgeous
TALENTED AND FABULOUS

GOOD MORNING *gorgeous!*

I AM GRATEFUL FOR

MY MANTRA
for today!

FUN!!! TODAY FOR FUN I WILL

☐ VISUALIZATION – SET YOUR TIMER FOR A MINIMUM OF 5 MINUTES AND GO THERE!

☐ MEDITATION – SET YOUR TIMER FOR A MINIMUM OF 5 MINUTES AND BE PRESENT, IN THE NOW. BREATHE.

☐ EXERCISE – DID YOU MOVE AT LEAST 30 MINUTES TODAY?

☐ FUEL – EAT 80% NUTRIENT DENSE FOOD THAT ENERGIZES YOU

I WAS MOST GRATEFUL FOR TODAY

Good Evening Gorgeous!

I LOVE TO GIVE. TODAY I GAVE

CHEERS TO ME!!!
LET'S CELEBRATE MY SUCCESSES FOR THE DAY

TODAY
is the best day
EVER !!!

DATE:

NOTES

------

1. ------
2. ------
3. ------

my top 3 goals for today that will lead me to joy

6AM – 9AM

10AM – 1PM

2PM – 5PM

6PM – 9PM

10PM – 6AM

make sure you get your sleep!

I AM BRILLIANT
gorgeous
TALENTED AND FABULOUS

GOOD MORNING *gorgeous!*

I AM GRATEFUL FOR

MY MANTRA

for today!

FUN!!! TODAY FOR FUN I WILL

- ☐ VISUALIZATION – SET YOUR TIMER FOR A MINIMUM OF 5 MINUTES AND GO THERE!
- ☐ MEDITATION – SET YOUR TIMER FOR A MINIMUM OF 5 MINUTES AND BE PRESENT, IN THE NOW. BREATHE.
- ☐ EXERCISE – DID YOU MOVE AT LEAST 30 MINUTES TODAY?
- ☐ FUEL – EAT 80% NUTRIENT DENSE FOOD THAT ENERGIZES YOU

I WAS MOST GRATEFUL FOR TODAY

Good Evening Gorgeous!

I LOVE TO GIVE. TODAY I GAVE

CHEERS TO ME!!!
LET'S CELEBRATE MY SUCCESSES FOR THE DAY

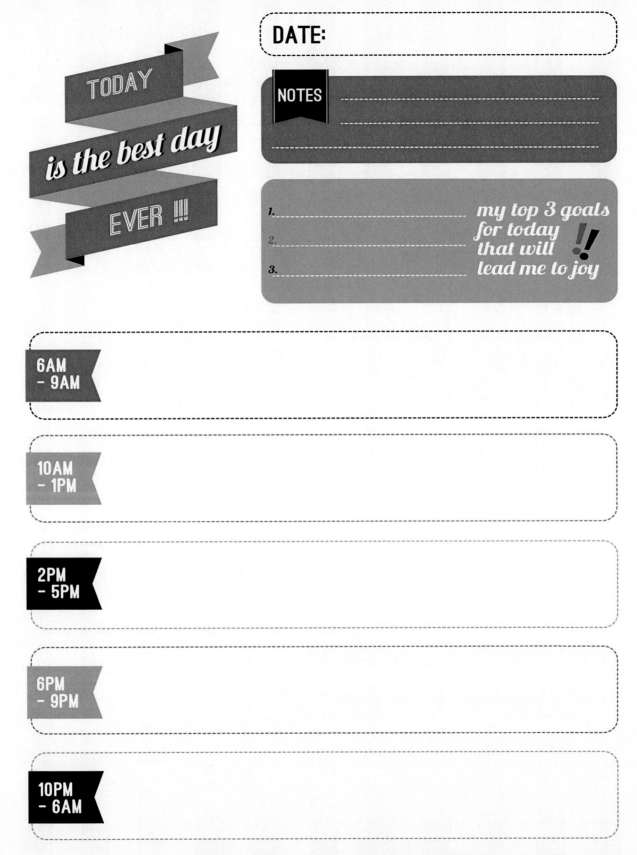

TODAY

is the best day

EVER !!!

DATE:

NOTES

1.
2.
3.

my top 3 goals for today that will lead me to joy

6AM – 9AM

10AM – 1PM

2PM – 5PM

6PM – 9PM

10PM – 6AM

make sure you get your sleep!

I AM BRILLIANT
gorgeous
TALENTED AND FABULOUS

GOOD MORNING *gorgeous!*

I AM GRATEFUL FOR

MY MANTRA
for today!

FUN!!! TODAY FOR FUN I WILL

- [ ] VISUALIZATION – SET YOUR TIMER FOR A MINIMUM OF 5 MINUTES AND GO THERE!
- [ ] MEDITATION – SET YOUR TIMER FOR A MINIMUM OF 5 MINUTES AND BE PRESENT, IN THE NOW. BREATHE.
- [ ] EXERCISE – DID YOU MOVE AT LEAST 30 MINUTES TODAY?
- [ ] FUEL – EAT 80% NUTRIENT DENSE FOOD THAT ENERGIZES YOU

I WAS MOST GRATEFUL FOR TODAY

Good Evening Gorgeous!

I LOVE TO GIVE. TODAY I GAVE

CHEERS TO ME!!!
LET'S CELEBRATE MY SUCCESSES FOR THE DAY

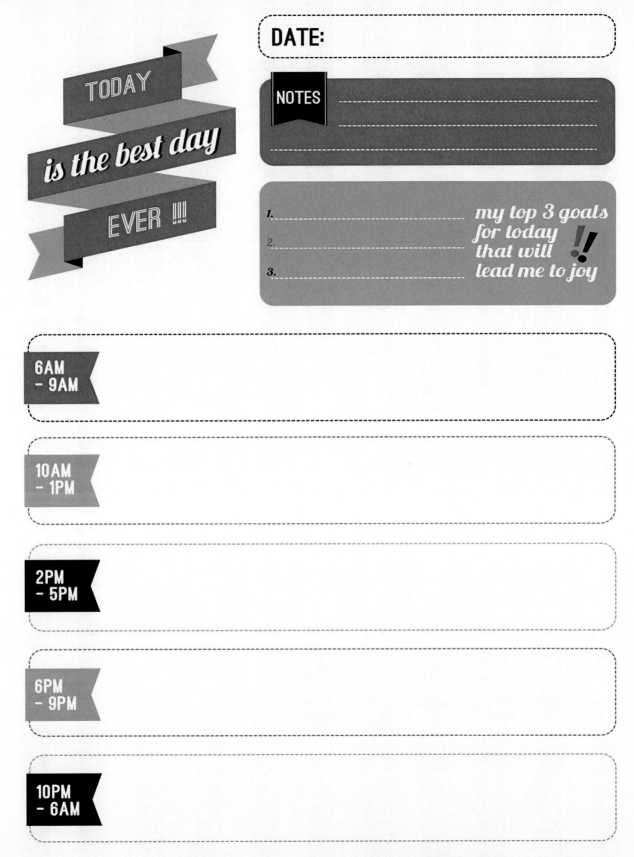

TODAY *is the best day* EVER !!!

DATE: _____

NOTES --

----

1. -
2. -
3. -

my top 3 goals for today that will lead me to joy ‼️

6AM – 9AM

10AM – 1PM

2PM – 5PM

6PM – 9PM

10PM – 6AM

make sure you get your sleep!

I AM BRILLIANT
gorgeous
TALENTED AND FABULOUS

GOOD MORNING *gorgeous!*

I AM GRATEFUL FOR

....
....
....

MY MANTRA

for today!

....
....
....

FUN!!! TODAY FOR FUN I WILL

....
....
....

☐ VISUALIZATION – SET YOUR TIMER FOR A MINIMUM OF 5 MINUTES AND GO THERE!

☐ MEDITATION – SET YOUR TIMER FOR A MINIMUM OF 5 MINUTES AND BE PRESENT, IN THE NOW. BREATHE.

☐ EXERCISE – DID YOU MOVE AT LEAST 30 MINUTES TODAY?

☐ FUEL – EAT 80% NUTRIENT DENSE FOOD THAT ENERGIZES YOU

I WAS MOST GRATEFUL FOR TODAY

....
....
....
....
....
....

Good Evening Gorgeous!

I LOVE TO GIVE. TODAY I GAVE

....
....
....

CHEERS TO ME!!!
LET'S CELEBRATE MY SUCCESSES FOR THE DAY

....
....
....

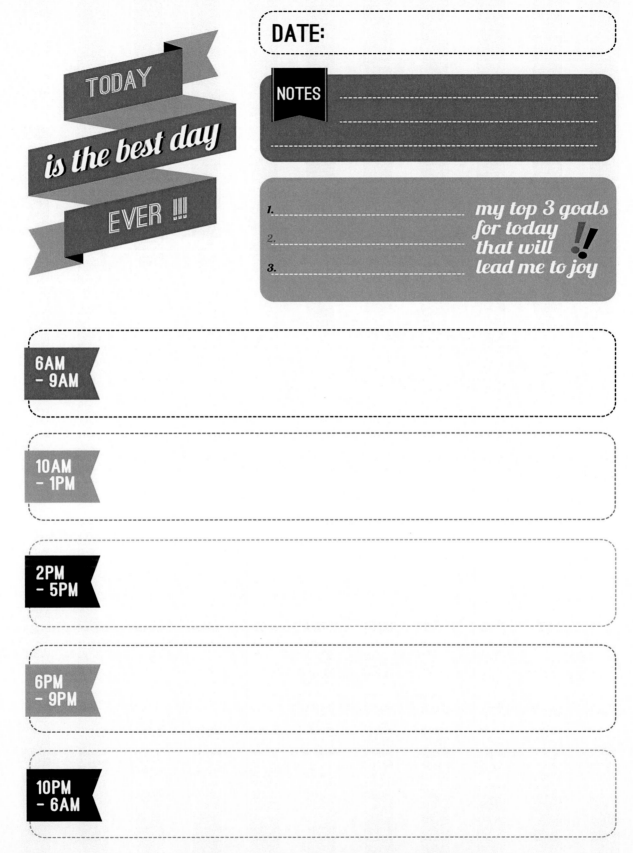

TODAY is the best day EVER !!!

DATE:

NOTES

1.
2.
3.

my top 3 goals
for today
that will
lead me to joy

6AM - 9AM

10AM - 1PM

2PM - 5PM

6PM - 9PM

10PM - 6AM

*make sure you get your sleep!

I AM BRILLIANT
gorgeous
TALENTED AND FABULOUS

GOOD MORNING
gorgeous!

I AM GRATEFUL FOR

MY MANTRA

for today!

FUN!!! TODAY FOR FUN I WILL

- VISUALIZATION – SET YOUR TIMER FOR A MINIMUM OF 5 MINUTES AND GO THERE!
- MEDITATION – SET YOUR TIMER FOR A MINIMUM OF 5 MINUTES AND BE PRESENT, IN THE NOW. BREATHE.
- EXERCISE – DID YOU MOVE AT LEAST 30 MINUTES TODAY?
- FUEL – EAT 80% NUTRIENT DENSE FOOD THAT ENERGIZES YOU

I WAS MOST GRATEFUL FOR TODAY

Good Evening Gorgeous!

I LOVE TO GIVE.
TODAY I GAVE

CHEERS TO ME!!!
LET'S CELEBRATE MY SUCCESSES FOR THE DAY

DATE:

NOTES ------------------------------

----

1. ------------------------------
2. ------------------------------
3. ------------------------------

*my top 3 goals
for today
that will
lead me to joy*

6AM – 9AM

10AM – 1PM

2PM – 5PM

6PM – 9PM

10PM – 6AM

make sure you get your sleep!

I AM BRILLIANT
gorgeous
TALENTED AND FABULOUS

GOOD MORNING
gorgeous!

I AM GRATEFUL FOR

MY MANTRA

for today!

FUN!!! TODAY FOR FUN I WILL

- [ ] VISUALIZATION - SET YOUR TIMER FOR A MINIMUM OF 5 MINUTES AND GO THERE!
- [ ] MEDITATION - SET YOUR TIMER FOR A MINIMUM OF 5 MINUTES AND BE PRESENT, IN THE NOW. BREATHE.
- [ ] EXERCISE - DID YOU MOVE AT LEAST 30 MINUTES TODAY?
- [ ] FUEL - EAT 80% NUTRIENT DENSE FOOD THAT ENERGIZES YOU

I WAS MOST GRATEFUL FOR TODAY

Good Evening Gorgeous!

I LOVE TO GIVE.
TODAY I GAVE

CHEERS TO ME!!!
LET'S CELEBRATE MY SUCCESSES FOR THE DAY

TODAY is the best day EVER !!!

DATE:

NOTES

1. ....
2. ....
3. ....

my top 3 goals for today that will lead me to joy !!

6AM – 9AM

10AM – 1PM

2PM – 5PM

6PM – 9PM

10PM – 6AM

*make sure you get your sleep!

I AM BRILLIANT
gorgeous
TALENTED AND FABULOUS

GOOD MORNING *gorgeous!*

I AM GRATEFUL FOR

MY MANTRA *for today!*

FUN!!! TODAY FOR FUN I WILL

- [ ] VISUALIZATION - SET YOUR TIMER FOR A MINIMUM OF 5 MINUTES AND GO THERE!
- [ ] MEDITATION - SET YOUR TIMER FOR A MINIMUM OF 5 MINUTES AND BE PRESENT, IN THE NOW. BREATHE.
- [ ] EXERCISE - DID YOU MOVE AT LEAST 30 MINUTES TODAY?
- [ ] FUEL - EAT 80% NUTRIENT DENSE FOOD THAT ENERGIZES YOU

I WAS MOST GRATEFUL FOR TODAY

Good Evening Gorgeous!

I LOVE TO GIVE. TODAY I GAVE

CHEERS TO ME!!!
LET'S CELEBRATE MY SUCCESSES FOR THE DAY

TODAY
is the best day
EVER !!!

DATE:

NOTES

1.
2.
3.

*my top 3 goals
for today
that will
lead me to joy*

6AM – 9AM

10AM – 1PM

2PM – 5PM

6PM – 9PM

10PM – 6AM

make sure you get your sleep!

I AM BRILLIANT
gorgeous
TALENTED AND FABULOUS

GOOD MORNING
gorgeous!

I AM GRATEFUL FOR

MY MANTRA
for today!

FUN!!! TODAY FOR FUN I WILL

- ☐ VISUALIZATION - SET YOUR TIMER FOR A MINIMUM OF 5 MINUTES AND GO THERE!
- ☐ MEDITATION - SET YOUR TIMER FOR A MINIMUM OF 5 MINUTES AND BE PRESENT, IN THE NOW. BREATHE.
- ☐ EXERCISE - DID YOU MOVE AT LEAST 30 MINUTES TODAY?
- ☐ FUEL - EAT 80% NUTRIENT DENSE FOOD THAT ENERGIZES YOU

Good Evening Gorgeous!

I WAS MOST GRATEFUL FOR TODAY

I LOVE TO GIVE.
TODAY I GAVE

CHEERS TO ME!!!
LET'S CELEBRATE MY SUCCESSES FOR THE DAY

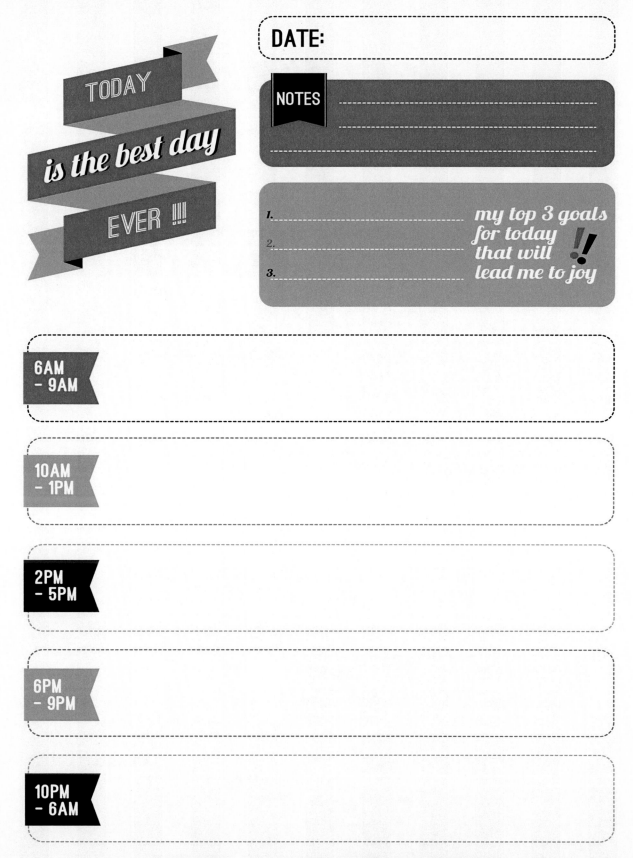

TODAY
is the best day
EVER !!!

DATE:

NOTES --

----

1. --
2. --
3. --

my top 3 goals
for today
that will
lead me to joy

6AM
– 9AM

10AM
– 1PM

2PM
– 5PM

6PM
– 9PM

10PM
– 6AM

*make sure you get your sleep!

I AM BRILLIANT
gorgeous
TALENTED AND FABULOUS

GOOD MORNING *gorgeous!*

I AM GRATEFUL FOR

MY MANTRA

for today!

FUN!!! TODAY FOR FUN I WILL

- [ ] VISUALIZATION - SET YOUR TIMER FOR A MINIMUM OF 5 MINUTES AND GO THERE!
- [ ] MEDITATION - SET YOUR TIMER FOR A MINIMUM OF 5 MINUTES AND BE PRESENT, IN THE NOW. BREATHE.
- [ ] EXERCISE - DID YOU MOVE AT LEAST 30 MINUTES TODAY?
- [ ] FUEL - EAT 80% NUTRIENT DENSE FOOD THAT ENERGIZES YOU

I WAS MOST GRATEFUL FOR TODAY

Good Evening Gorgeous!

I LOVE TO GIVE. TODAY I GAVE

CHEERS TO ME!!!
LET'S CELEBRATE MY SUCCESSES FOR THE DAY

TODAY is the best day EVER !!!

DATE:

NOTES

1.
2.
3.

my top 3 goals for today that will lead me to joy !!

6AM – 9AM

10AM – 1PM

2PM – 5PM

6PM – 9PM

10PM – 6AM

*make sure you get your sleep!

I AM BRILLIANT
gorgeous
TALENTED AND FABULOUS

GOOD MORNING *gorgeous!*

I AM GRATEFUL FOR

MY MANTRA

for today!

FUN!!! TODAY FOR FUN I WILL

☐ VISUALIZATION – SET YOUR TIMER FOR A MINIMUM OF 5 MINUTES AND GO THERE!

☐ MEDITATION – SET YOUR TIMER FOR A MINIMUM OF 5 MINUTES AND BE PRESENT, IN THE NOW. BREATHE.

☐ EXERCISE – DID YOU MOVE AT LEAST 30 MINUTES TODAY?

☐ FUEL – EAT 80% NUTRIENT DENSE FOOD THAT ENERGIZES YOU

I WAS MOST GRATEFUL FOR TODAY

Good Evening Gorgeous!

I LOVE TO GIVE. TODAY I GAVE

CHEERS TO ME!!!
LET'S CELEBRATE MY SUCCESSES FOR THE DAY

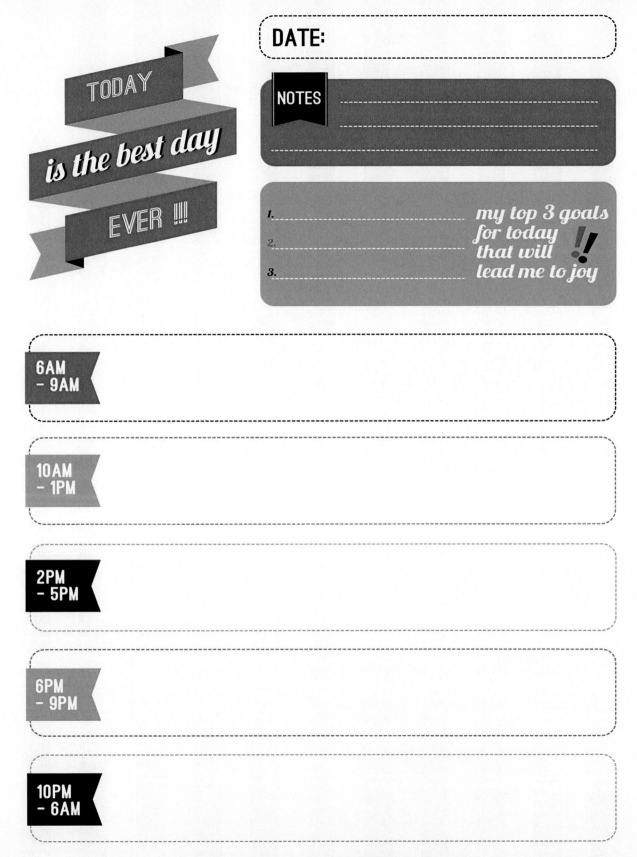

TODAY is the best day EVER !!!

DATE:

NOTES

1.
2.
3.

*my top 3 goals
for today
that will
lead me to joy*

6AM – 9AM

10AM – 1PM

2PM – 5PM

6PM – 9PM

10PM – 6AM

make sure you get your sleep!

I AM BRILLIANT
gorgeous
TALENTED AND FABULOUS

GOOD MORNING
gorgeous!

I AM GRATEFUL FOR

MY MANTRA

for today!

- - - - - - - - - - - - - - - - - -

- - - - - - - - - - - - - - - - - -

- - - - - - - - - - - - - - - - - -

FUN!!! TODAY FOR FUN I WILL

....

....

....

☐ VISUALIZATION – SET YOUR TIMER FOR A MINIMUM OF 5 MINUTES AND GO THERE!

☐ MEDITATION – SET YOUR TIMER FOR A MINIMUM OF 5 MINUTES AND BE PRESENT, IN THE NOW. BREATHE.

☐ EXERCISE – DID YOU MOVE AT LEAST 30 MINUTES TODAY?

☐ FUEL – EAT 80% NUTRIENT DENSE FOOD THAT ENERGIZES YOU

I WAS MOST GRATEFUL FOR TODAY

- - - - - - - - - - - - - - - - - - - -

- - - - - - - - - - - - - - - - - - - -

- - - - - - - - - - - - - - - - - - - -

- - - - - - - - - - - - - - - - - - - -

- - - - - - - - - - - - - - - - - - - -

- - - - - - - - - - - - - - - - - - - -

Good Evening Gorgeous!

I LOVE TO GIVE.
TODAY I GAVE

- - - - - - - - - - - - - - - - - -

- - - - - - - - - - - - - - - - - -

- - - - - - - - - - - - - - - - - -

CHEERS TO ME!!!
LET'S CELEBRATE MY SUCCESSES FOR THE DAY

- -

- -

- -

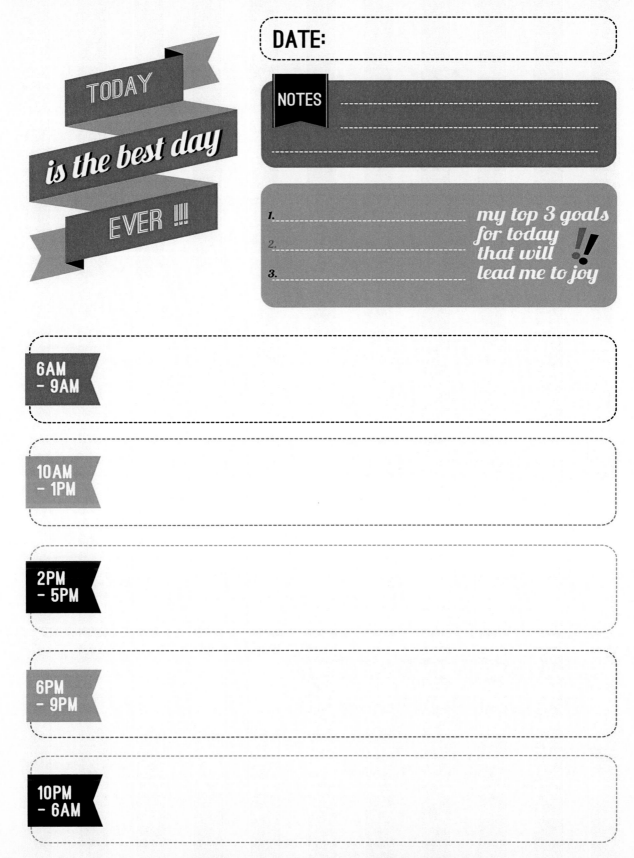

TODAY
is the best day
EVER !!!

DATE:

NOTES

----

1. --------------------------------
2. --------------------------------
3. --------------------------------

my top 3 goals
for today
that will
lead me to joy

6AM – 9AM

10AM – 1PM

2PM – 5PM

6PM – 9PM

10PM – 6AM

*make sure you get your sleep!

I AM BRILLIANT
gorgeous
TALENTED AND FABULOUS

GOOD MORNING *gorgeous!*

I AM GRATEFUL FOR

....

....

....

MY MANTRA

for today!

....

....

....

....

FUN!!! TODAY FOR FUN I WILL

....

....

....

☐ VISUALIZATION - SET YOUR TIMER FOR A MINIMUM OF 5 MINUTES AND GO THERE!

☐ MEDITATION - SET YOUR TIMER FOR A MINIMUM OF 5 MINUTES AND BE PRESENT, IN THE NOW. BREATHE.

☐ EXERCISE - DID YOU MOVE AT LEAST 30 MINUTES TODAY?

☐ FUEL - EAT 80% NUTRIENT DENSE FOOD THAT ENERGIZES YOU

I WAS MOST GRATEFUL FOR TODAY

....

....

....

....

....

....

Good Evening Gorgeous!

I LOVE TO GIVE.
TODAY I GAVE

....

....

....

CHEERS TO ME!!!
LET'S CELEBRATE MY SUCCESSES FOR THE DAY

....

....

....

....

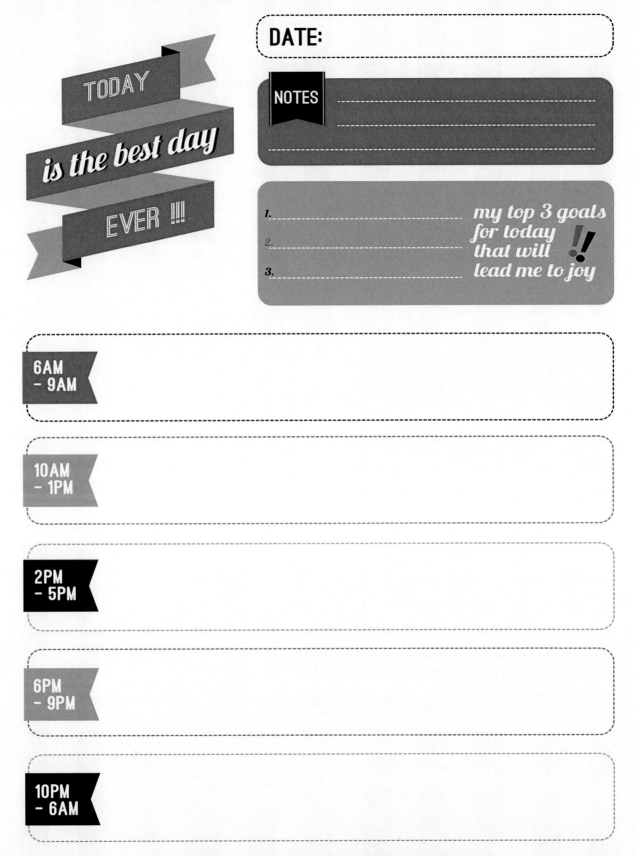

TODAY
is the best day
EVER !!!

DATE:

NOTES --

----

1. --
2. --
3. --

*my top 3 goals
for today
that will
lead me to joy*

6AM – 9AM

10AM – 1PM

2PM – 5PM

6PM – 9PM

10PM – 6AM

make sure you get your sleep!

I AM BRILLIANT
gorgeous
TALENTED AND FABULOUS

GOOD MORNING *gorgeous!*

I AM GRATEFUL FOR

MY MANTRA

for today!

FUN!!! TODAY FOR FUN I WILL

- [ ] VISUALIZATION – SET YOUR TIMER FOR A MINIMUM OF 5 MINUTES AND GO THERE!
- [ ] MEDITATION – SET YOUR TIMER FOR A MINIMUM OF 5 MINUTES AND BE PRESENT, IN THE NOW. BREATHE.
- [ ] EXERCISE – DID YOU MOVE AT LEAST 30 MINUTES TODAY?
- [ ] FUEL – EAT 80% NUTRIENT DENSE FOOD THAT ENERGIZES YOU

I WAS MOST GRATEFUL FOR TODAY

Good Evening Gorgeous!

I LOVE TO GIVE.
TODAY I GAVE

CHEERS TO ME!!!
LET'S CELEBRATE MY SUCCESSES FOR THE DAY

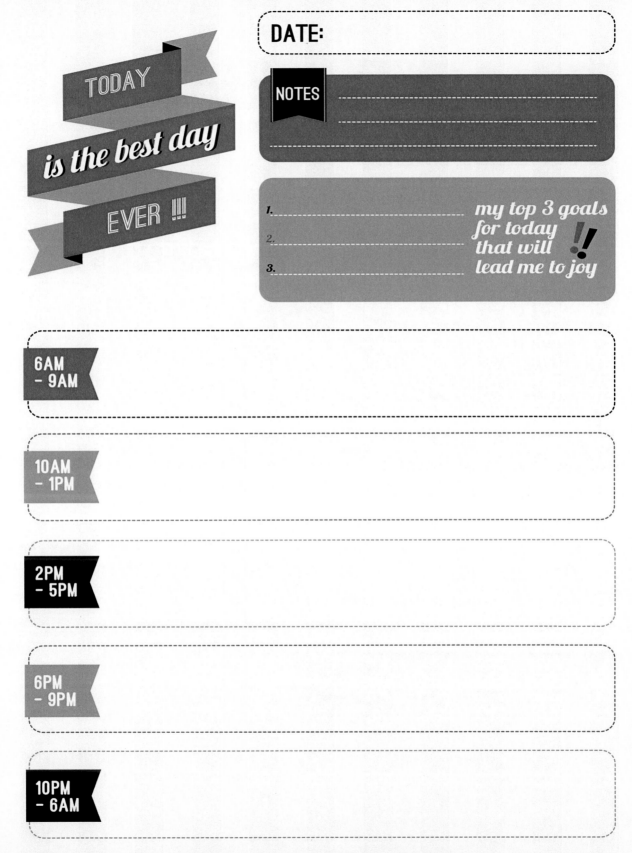

TODAY **is the best day** EVER !!!

DATE:

NOTES

1.
2.
3.

my top 3 goals
for today
that will
lead me to joy

6AM – 9AM

10AM – 1PM

2PM – 5PM

6PM – 9PM

10PM – 6AM

*make sure you get your sleep!

I AM BRILLIANT
gorgeous
TALENTED AND FABULOUS

GOOD MORNING *gorgeous!*

I AM GRATEFUL FOR

MY MANTRA *for today!*

FUN!!! TODAY FOR FUN I WILL

- ☐ VISUALIZATION - SET YOUR TIMER FOR A MINIMUM OF 5 MINUTES AND GO THERE!
- ☐ MEDITATION - SET YOUR TIMER FOR A MINIMUM OF 5 MINUTES AND BE PRESENT, IN THE NOW. BREATHE.
- ☐ EXERCISE - DID YOU MOVE AT LEAST 30 MINUTES TODAY?
- ☐ FUEL - EAT 80% NUTRIENT DENSE FOOD THAT ENERGIZES YOU

I WAS MOST GRATEFUL FOR TODAY

Good Evening Gorgeous!

I LOVE TO GIVE. TODAY I GAVE

CHEERS TO ME!!!
LET'S CELEBRATE MY SUCCESSES FOR THE DAY

TODAY is the best day EVER !!!

DATE:

NOTES

1.
2.
3.

my top 3 goals for today that will lead me to joy

6AM – 9AM

10AM – 1PM

2PM – 5PM

6PM – 9PM

10PM – 6AM

make sure you get your sleep!

PAUSE CAFÉ

coffee break 〝

time to pause and reflect. are you focused on your goals? need to revise your priorities? get more specific with your visualization? add some new mantras? grab a cup of hot coffee or tea and sit down and focus on your joyful plan for the next 30 days.

L'ART DE VIVRE!

VISUALIZE THE NEXT 30 DAYS

RAISON D'ÊTRE!

WHAT ARE YOUR TOP 2-3 PRIORITIES?

PAIN AU CHOCOLAT

FOR YOUR BRAIN!

MANTRAS AND AFFIRMATIONS YOU NEED TO HEAR DAILY

LA VIE EST BELLE!

WHAT ARE YOU MOST GRATEFUL FOR FROM THE LAST 30 DAYS?

VIVRE LA VIE PAR LA CONCEPTION!

REVISIT YOUR 10 GOALS FOR THE YEAR

(THINGS CHANGE, PERSPECTIVE, PRIORITIES OR MAYBE YOU ACCOMPLISHED A GOAL AND WOULD LIKE TO ADD ANOTHER. OR, MAYBE THEY ARE THE SAME AND YOU NEED TO REWRITE THEM HERE)

I AM BRILLIANT
gorgeous
TALENTED AND FABULOUS

GOOD MORNING gorgeous!

I AM GRATEFUL FOR

MY MANTRA

for today!

FUN!!! TODAY FOR FUN I WILL

☐ VISUALIZATION – SET YOUR TIMER FOR A MINIMUM OF 5 MINUTES AND GO THERE!

☐ MEDITATION – SET YOUR TIMER FOR A MINIMUM OF 5 MINUTES AND BE PRESENT, IN THE NOW. BREATHE.

☐ EXERCISE – DID YOU MOVE AT LEAST 30 MINUTES TODAY?

☐ FUEL – EAT 80% NUTRIENT DENSE FOOD THAT ENERGIZES YOU

I WAS MOST GRATEFUL FOR TODAY

Good Evening Gorgeous!

I LOVE TO GIVE.
TODAY I GAVE

CHEERS TO ME!!!
LET'S CELEBRATE MY SUCCESSES FOR THE DAY

TODAY
is the best day
EVER !!!

DATE:

NOTES _____
_____
_____

1. _____
2. _____
3. _____

my top 3 goals
for today
that will
lead me to joy

6AM
– 9AM

10AM
– 1PM

2PM
– 5PM

6PM
– 9PM

10PM
– 6AM

*make sure you get your sleep!

I AM BRILLIANT
gorgeous
TALENTED AND FABULOUS

GOOD MORNING *gorgeous!*

I AM GRATEFUL FOR
....
....
....

MY MANTRA

for today!

....
....
....

FUN!!! TODAY FOR FUN I WILL
....
....
....

☐ VISUALIZATION – SET YOUR TIMER FOR A MINIMUM OF 5 MINUTES AND GO THERE!

☐ MEDITATION – SET YOUR TIMER FOR A MINIMUM OF 5 MINUTES AND BE PRESENT, IN THE NOW. BREATHE.

☐ EXERCISE – DID YOU MOVE AT LEAST 30 MINUTES TODAY?

☐ FUEL – EAT 80% NUTRIENT DENSE FOOD THAT ENERGIZES YOU

I WAS MOST GRATEFUL FOR TODAY
....
....
....
....
....
....

Good Evening Gorgeous!

I LOVE TO GIVE. TODAY I GAVE
....
....
....

CHEERS TO ME!!!
LET'S CELEBRATE MY SUCCESSES FOR THE DAY
....
....
....

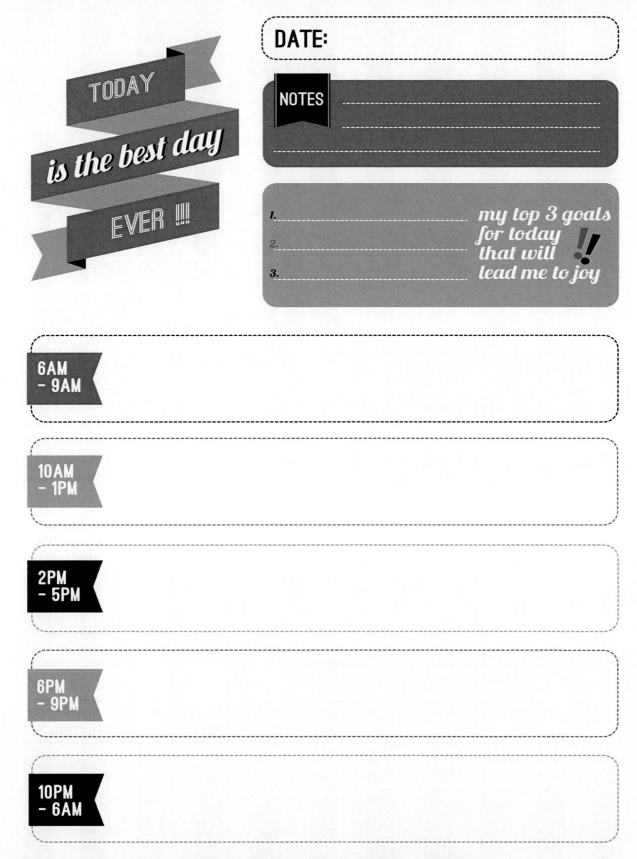

TODAY

is the best day

EVER !!!

DATE:

NOTES

1.
2.
3.

my top 3 goals for today that will lead me to joy !!

6AM – 9AM

10AM – 1PM

2PM – 5PM

6PM – 9PM

10PM – 6AM

make sure you get your sleep!

I AM BRILLIANT
gorgeous
TALENTED AND FABULOUS

GOOD MORNING *gorgeous!*

I AM GRATEFUL FOR

MY MANTRA *for today!*

FUN!!! TODAY FOR FUN I WILL

- ☐ VISUALIZATION – SET YOUR TIMER FOR A MINIMUM OF 5 MINUTES AND GO THERE!
- ☐ MEDITATION – SET YOUR TIMER FOR A MINIMUM OF 5 MINUTES AND BE PRESENT, IN THE NOW. BREATHE.
- ☐ EXERCISE – DID YOU MOVE AT LEAST 30 MINUTES TODAY?
- ☐ FUEL – EAT 80% NUTRIENT DENSE FOOD THAT ENERGIZES YOU

I WAS MOST GRATEFUL FOR TODAY

Good Evening Gorgeous!

I LOVE TO GIVE. TODAY I GAVE

CHEERS TO ME!!!
LET'S CELEBRATE MY SUCCESSES FOR THE DAY

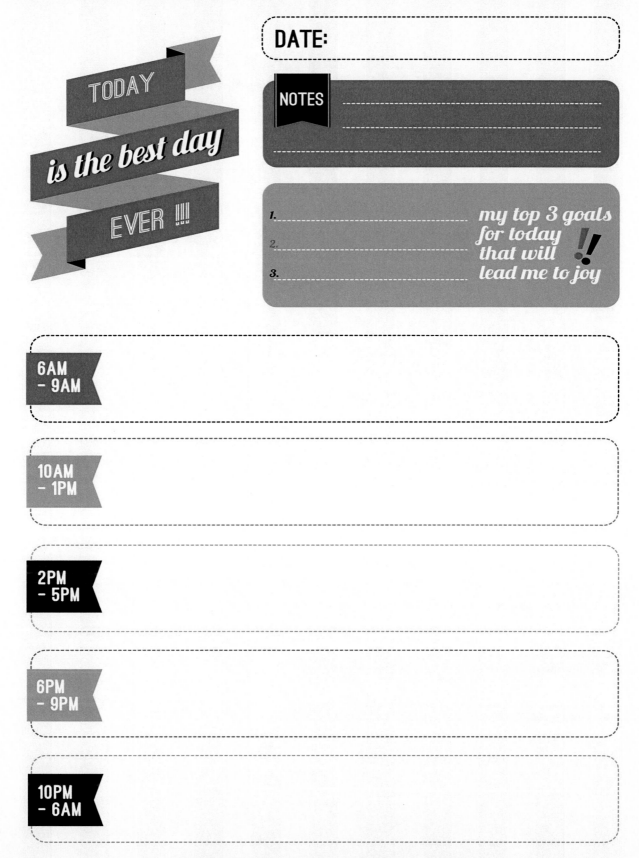

TODAY
is the best day
EVER !!!

DATE:

NOTES

1.
2.
3.
my top 3 goals
for today
that will
lead me to joy

6AM
– 9AM

10AM
– 1PM

2PM
– 5PM

6PM
– 9PM

10PM
– 6AM

*make sure you get your sleep!

I AM BRILLIANT
gorgeous
TALENTED AND FABULOUS

GOOD MORNING *gorgeous!*

I AM GRATEFUL FOR

MY MANTRA *for today!*

FUN!!! TODAY FOR FUN I WILL

☐ VISUALIZATION – SET YOUR TIMER FOR A MINIMUM OF 5 MINUTES AND GO THERE!

☐ MEDITATION – SET YOUR TIMER FOR A MINIMUM OF 5 MINUTES AND BE PRESENT, IN THE NOW. BREATHE.

☐ EXERCISE – DID YOU MOVE AT LEAST 30 MINUTES TODAY?

☐ FUEL – EAT 80% NUTRIENT DENSE FOOD THAT ENERGIZES YOU

I WAS MOST GRATEFUL FOR TODAY

Good Evening Gorgeous!

I LOVE TO GIVE. TODAY I GAVE

CHEERS TO ME!!!
LET'S CELEBRATE MY SUCCESSES FOR THE DAY

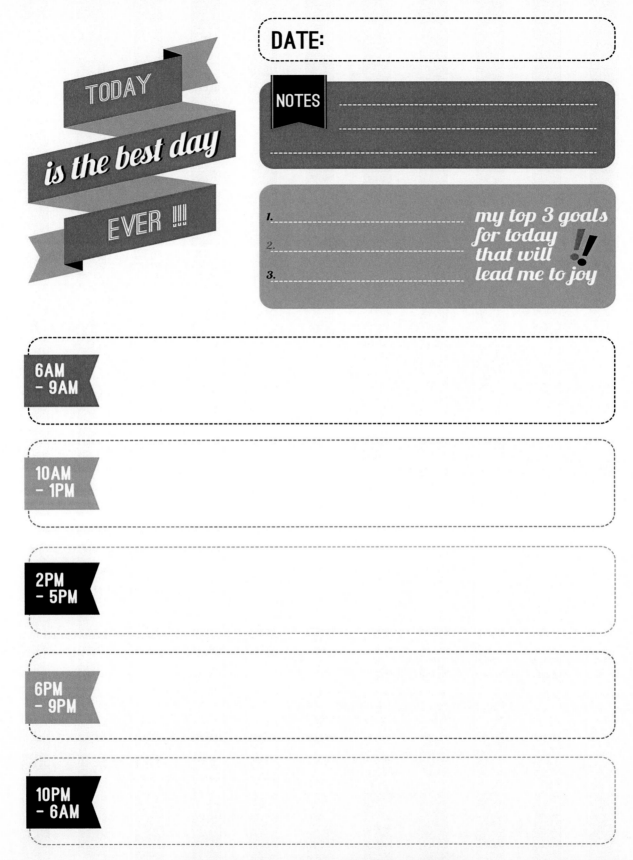

TODAY
is the best day
EVER !!!

DATE:

NOTES

1.
2.
3.

my top 3 goals
for today
that will
lead me to joy

6AM
– 9AM

10AM
– 1PM

2PM
– 5PM

6PM
– 9PM

10PM
– 6AM

*make sure you get your sleep!

I AM BRILLIANT
gorgeous
TALENTED AND FABULOUS

GOOD MORNING *gorgeous!*

I AM GRATEFUL FOR

MY MANTRA

for today!

FUN!!! TODAY FOR FUN I WILL

☐ VISUALIZATION – SET YOUR TIMER FOR A MINIMUM OF 5 MINUTES AND GO THERE!

☐ MEDITATION – SET YOUR TIMER FOR A MINIMUM OF 5 MINUTES AND BE PRESENT, IN THE NOW. BREATHE.

☐ EXERCISE – DID YOU MOVE AT LEAST 30 MINUTES TODAY?

☐ FUEL – EAT 80% NUTRIENT DENSE FOOD THAT ENERGIZES YOU

I WAS MOST GRATEFUL FOR TODAY

Good Evening Gorgeous!

I LOVE TO GIVE.
TODAY I GAVE

CHEERS TO ME!!!
LET'S CELEBRATE MY SUCCESSES FOR THE DAY

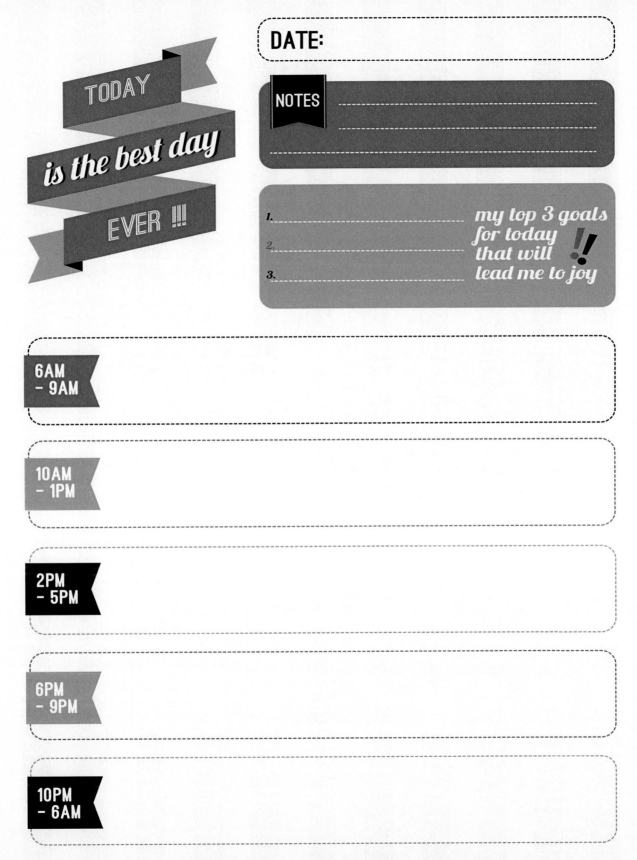

DATE:

NOTES --

TODAY is the best day EVER !!!

1. ------------------------------------
2. ------------------------------------
3. ------------------------------------

my top 3 goals for today that will lead me to joy

6AM – 9AM

10AM – 1PM

2PM – 5PM

6PM – 9PM

10PM – 6AM

*make sure you get your sleep!

I AM BRILLIANT
gorgeous
TALENTED AND FABULOUS

GOOD MORNING *gorgeous!*

I AM GRATEFUL FOR

MY MANTRA *for today!*

FUN!!! TODAY FOR FUN I WILL

☐ VISUALIZATION – SET YOUR TIMER FOR A MINIMUM OF 5 MINUTES AND GO THERE!

☐ MEDITATION – SET YOUR TIMER FOR A MINIMUM OF 5 MINUTES AND BE PRESENT, IN THE NOW. BREATHE.

☐ EXERCISE – DID YOU MOVE AT LEAST 30 MINUTES TODAY?

☐ FUEL – EAT 80% NUTRIENT DENSE FOOD THAT ENERGIZES YOU

I WAS MOST GRATEFUL FOR TODAY

Good Evening Gorgeous!

I LOVE TO GIVE. TODAY I GAVE

CHEERS TO ME!!!
LET'S CELEBRATE MY SUCCESSES FOR THE DAY

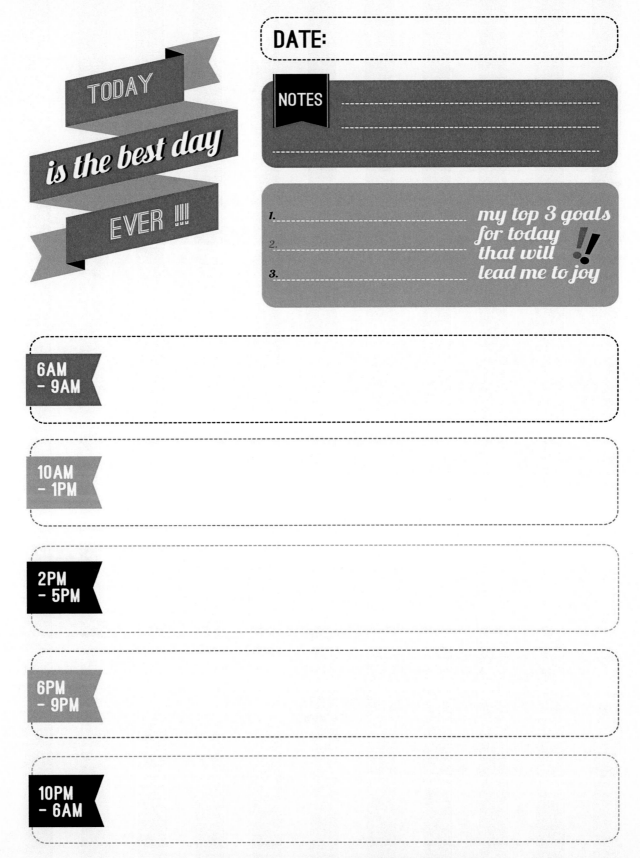

TODAY

is the best day

EVER !!!

DATE:

NOTES

1.
2.
3.

my top 3 goals
for today
that will
lead me to joy

6AM
– 9AM

10AM
– 1PM

2PM
– 5PM

6PM
– 9PM

10PM
– 6AM

make sure you get your sleep!

I AM BRILLIANT
gorgeous
TALENTED AND FABULOUS

GOOD MORNING
gorgeous!

I AM GRATEFUL FOR

MY MANTRA

for today!

FUN!!! TODAY FOR FUN I WILL

- [ ] VISUALIZATION – SET YOUR TIMER FOR A MINIMUM OF 5 MINUTES AND GO THERE!
- [ ] MEDITATION – SET YOUR TIMER FOR A MINIMUM OF 5 MINUTES AND BE PRESENT, IN THE NOW. BREATHE.
- [ ] EXERCISE – DID YOU MOVE AT LEAST 30 MINUTES TODAY?
- [ ] FUEL – EAT 80% NUTRIENT DENSE FOOD THAT ENERGIZES YOU

I WAS MOST GRATEFUL FOR TODAY

Good Evening Gorgeous!

I LOVE TO GIVE.
TODAY I GAVE

CHEERS TO ME!!!
LET'S CELEBRATE MY SUCCESSES FOR THE DAY

TODAY *is the best day* **EVER !!!**

DATE:

NOTES
_____
_____
_____

1. _____
2. _____
3. _____

my top 3 goals for today that will lead me to joy

6AM – 9AM

10AM – 1PM

2PM – 5PM

6PM – 9PM

10PM – 6AM

make sure you get your sleep!

I AM BRILLIANT
gorgeous
TALENTED AND FABULOUS

GOOD MORNING *gorgeous!*

I AM GRATEFUL FOR

....
....
....

MY MANTRA

for today!

....
....
....
....

FUN!!! TODAY FOR FUN I WILL

....
....
....

- [ ] VISUALIZATION – SET YOUR TIMER FOR A MINIMUM OF 5 MINUTES AND GO THERE!
- [ ] MEDITATION – SET YOUR TIMER FOR A MINIMUM OF 5 MINUTES AND BE PRESENT, IN THE NOW. BREATHE.
- [ ] EXERCISE – DID YOU MOVE AT LEAST 30 MINUTES TODAY?
- [ ] FUEL – EAT 80% NUTRIENT DENSE FOOD THAT ENERGIZES YOU

I WAS MOST GRATEFUL FOR TODAY

....
....
....
....
....
....

Good Evening Gorgeous!

I LOVE TO GIVE.
TODAY I GAVE

....
....
....

CHEERS TO ME!!!
LET'S CELEBRATE MY SUCCESSES FOR THE DAY

....
....
....

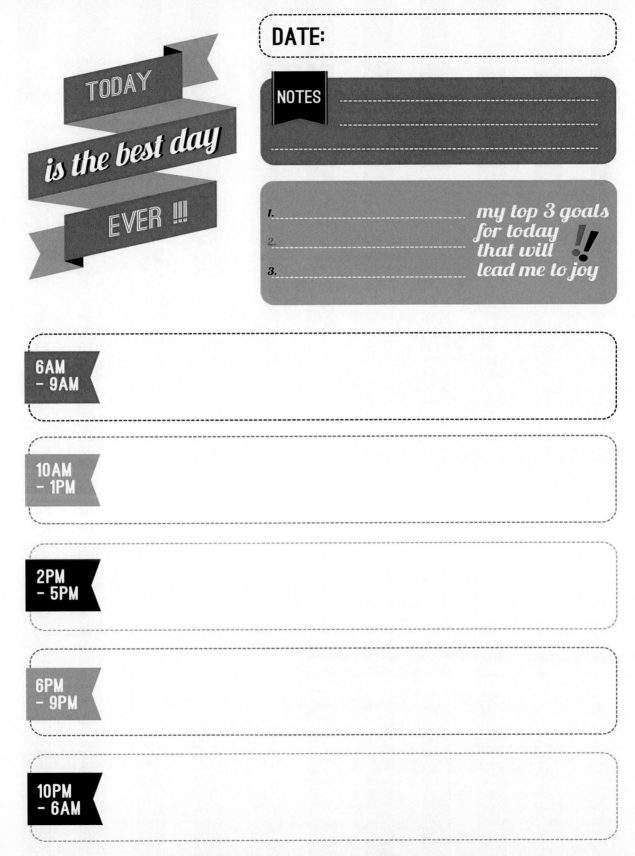

TODAY is the best day EVER !!!

DATE:

NOTES
- -
- -
- -

1. -
2. -
3. -

my top 3 goals for today that will lead me to joy

6AM – 9AM

10AM – 1PM

2PM – 5PM

6PM – 9PM

10PM – 6AM

make sure you get your sleep!

I AM BRILLIANT
gorgeous
TALENTED AND FABULOUS

GOOD MORNING *gorgeous!*

MY MANTRA *for today!*

....
....
....
....

I AM GRATEFUL FOR

....
....
....
....

FUN!!! TODAY FOR FUN I WILL

....
....
....

☐ VISUALIZATION - SET YOUR TIMER FOR A MINIMUM OF 5 MINUTES AND GO THERE!

☐ MEDITATION - SET YOUR TIMER FOR A MINIMUM OF 5 MINUTES AND BE PRESENT, IN THE NOW. BREATHE.

☐ EXERCISE - DID YOU MOVE AT LEAST 30 MINUTES TODAY?

☐ FUEL - EAT 80% NUTRIENT DENSE FOOD THAT ENERGIZES YOU

I WAS MOST GRATEFUL FOR TODAY

....
....
....
....
....
....

Good Evening Gorgeous!

I LOVE TO GIVE. TODAY I GAVE

....
....
....

CHEERS TO ME!!!
LET'S CELEBRATE MY SUCCESSES FOR THE DAY

....
....
....

TODAY

is the best day

EVER !!!

DATE:

NOTES ....
....
....

1. ....
2. ....
3. ....

*my top 3 goals
for today
that will* **!!**
lead me to joy

6AM
- 9AM

10AM
- 1PM

2PM
- 5PM

6PM
- 9PM

10PM
- 6AM

make sure you get your sleep!

I AM BRILLIANT
gorgeous
TALENTED AND FABULOUS

GOOD MORNING *gorgeous!*

I AM GRATEFUL FOR

MY MANTRA

for today!

FUN!!! TODAY FOR FUN I WILL

- [ ] VISUALIZATION – SET YOUR TIMER FOR A MINIMUM OF 5 MINUTES AND GO THERE!
- [ ] MEDITATION – SET YOUR TIMER FOR A MINIMUM OF 5 MINUTES AND BE PRESENT, IN THE NOW. BREATHE.
- [ ] EXERCISE – DID YOU MOVE AT LEAST 30 MINUTES TODAY?
- [ ] FUEL – EAT 80% NUTRIENT DENSE FOOD THAT ENERGIZES YOU

I WAS MOST GRATEFUL FOR TODAY

Good Evening Gorgeous!

I LOVE TO GIVE.
TODAY I GAVE

CHEERS TO ME!!!
LET'S CELEBRATE MY SUCCESSES FOR THE DAY

TODAY

is the best day

EVER !!!

DATE:

NOTES

1.
2.
3.

my top 3 goals for today that will lead me to joy !!

6AM – 9AM

10AM – 1PM

2PM – 5PM

6PM – 9PM

10PM – 6AM

make sure you get your sleep!

I AM BRILLIANT
gorgeous
TALENTED AND FABULOUS

GOOD MORNING *gorgeous!*

I AM GRATEFUL FOR

MY MANTRA

for today!

FUN!!! TODAY FOR FUN I WILL

- [ ] VISUALIZATION – SET YOUR TIMER FOR A MINIMUM OF 5 MINUTES AND GO THERE!
- [ ] MEDITATION – SET YOUR TIMER FOR A MINIMUM OF 5 MINUTES AND BE PRESENT, IN THE NOW. BREATHE.
- [ ] EXERCISE – DID YOU MOVE AT LEAST 30 MINUTES TODAY?
- [ ] FUEL – EAT 80% NUTRIENT DENSE FOOD THAT ENERGIZES YOU

I WAS MOST GRATEFUL FOR TODAY

Good Evening Gorgeous!

I LOVE TO GIVE.
TODAY I GAVE

CHEERS TO ME!!!
LET'S CELEBRATE MY SUCCESSES FOR THE DAY

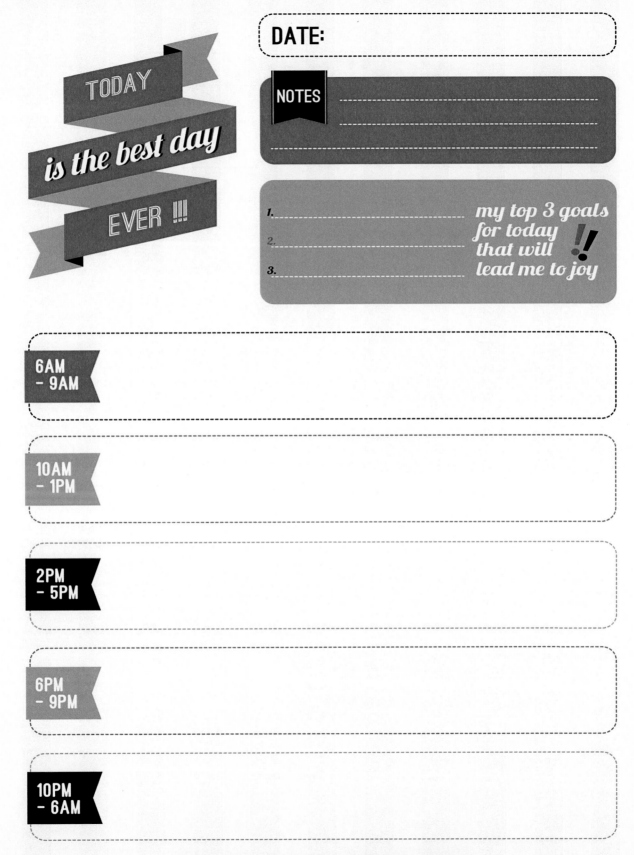

TODAY
is the best day
EVER !!!

DATE:

NOTES

1.
2.
3.

my top 3 goals
for today
that will
lead me to joy

6AM – 9AM

10AM – 1PM

2PM – 5PM

6PM – 9PM

10PM – 6AM

*make sure you get your sleep!

I AM BRILLIANT
gorgeous
TALENTED AND FABULOUS

GOOD MORNING *gorgeous!*

I AM GRATEFUL FOR

MY MANTRA

for today!

FUN!!! TODAY FOR FUN I WILL

☐ VISUALIZATION – SET YOUR TIMER FOR A MINIMUM OF 5 MINUTES AND GO THERE!

☐ MEDITATION – SET YOUR TIMER FOR A MINIMUM OF 5 MINUTES AND BE PRESENT, IN THE NOW. BREATHE.

☐ EXERCISE – DID YOU MOVE AT LEAST 30 MINUTES TODAY?

☐ FUEL – EAT 80% NUTRIENT DENSE FOOD THAT ENERGIZES YOU

I WAS MOST GRATEFUL FOR TODAY

Good Evening Gorgeous!

I LOVE TO GIVE.
TODAY I GAVE

CHEERS TO ME!!!
LET'S CELEBRATE MY SUCCESSES FOR THE DAY

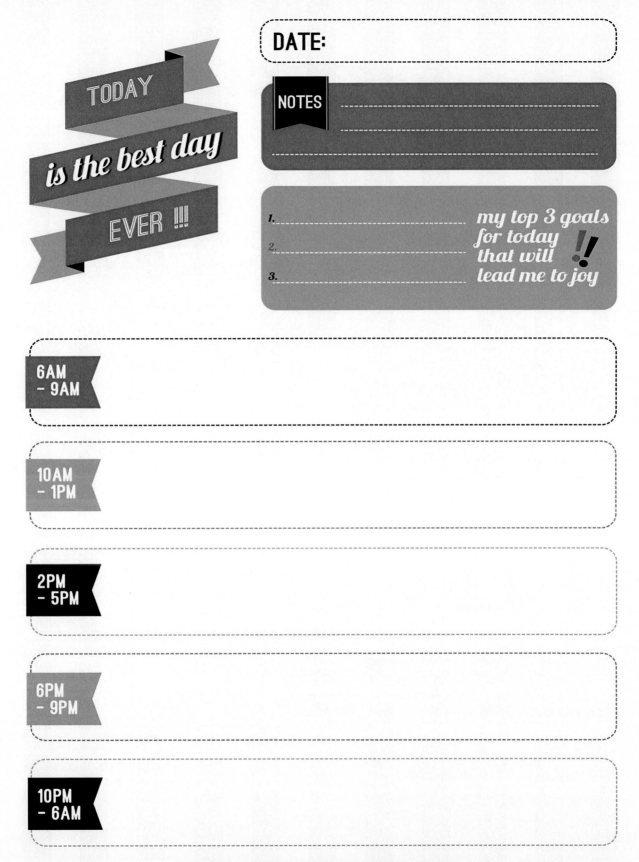

DATE:

NOTES

my top 3 goals
for today
that will
lead me to joy

1.
2.
3.

6AM – 9AM

10AM – 1PM

2PM – 5PM

6PM – 9PM

10PM – 6AM

*make sure you get your sleep!

I AM BRILLIANT
gorgeous
TALENTED AND FABULOUS

GOOD MORNING *gorgeous!*

I AM GRATEFUL FOR

MY MANTRA

for today!

FUN!!! TODAY FOR FUN I WILL

- [ ] VISUALIZATION – SET YOUR TIMER FOR A MINIMUM OF 5 MINUTES AND GO THERE!
- [ ] MEDITATION – SET YOUR TIMER FOR A MINIMUM OF 5 MINUTES AND BE PRESENT, IN THE NOW. BREATHE.
- [ ] EXERCISE – DID YOU MOVE AT LEAST 30 MINUTES TODAY?
- [ ] FUEL – EAT 80% NUTRIENT DENSE FOOD THAT ENERGIZES YOU

I WAS MOST GRATEFUL FOR TODAY

Good Evening Gorgeous!

I LOVE TO GIVE.
TODAY I GAVE

CHEERS TO ME!!!
LET'S CELEBRATE MY SUCCESSES FOR THE DAY

TODAY

is the best day

EVER !!!

DATE:

NOTES

1.
2.
3.

*my top 3 goals
for today
that will
lead me to joy*

6AM
– 9AM

10AM
– 1PM

2PM
– 5PM

6PM
– 9PM

10PM
– 6AM

make sure you get your sleep!

I AM BRILLIANT
gorgeous
TALENTED AND FABULOUS

GOOD MORNING *gorgeous!*

I AM GRATEFUL FOR

MY MANTRA

for today!

FUN!!! TODAY FOR FUN I WILL

☐ VISUALIZATION – SET YOUR TIMER FOR A MINIMUM OF 5 MINUTES AND GO THERE!

☐ MEDITATION – SET YOUR TIMER FOR A MINIMUM OF 5 MINUTES AND BE PRESENT, IN THE NOW. BREATHE.

☐ EXERCISE – DID YOU MOVE AT LEAST 30 MINUTES TODAY?

☐ FUEL – EAT 80% NUTRIENT DENSE FOOD THAT ENERGIZES YOU

I WAS MOST GRATEFUL FOR TODAY

Good Evening Gorgeous!

I LOVE TO GIVE.
TODAY I GAVE

CHEERS TO ME!!!
LET'S CELEBRATE MY SUCCESSES FOR THE DAY

TODAY

is the best day

EVER !!!

DATE:

NOTES

----

1. -
2. -
3. -

*my top 3 goals
for today
that will !!
lead me to joy*

6AM – 9AM

10AM – 1PM

2PM – 5PM

6PM – 9PM

10PM – 6AM

make sure you get your sleep!

I AM BRILLIANT
gorgeous
TALENTED AND FABULOUS

GOOD MORNING *gorgeous!*

I AM GRATEFUL FOR

MY MANTRA

for today!

FUN!!! TODAY FOR FUN I WILL

- ☐ VISUALIZATION – SET YOUR TIMER FOR A MINIMUM OF 5 MINUTES AND GO THERE!
- ☐ MEDITATION – SET YOUR TIMER FOR A MINIMUM OF 5 MINUTES AND BE PRESENT, IN THE NOW. BREATHE.
- ☐ EXERCISE – DID YOU MOVE AT LEAST 30 MINUTES TODAY?
- ☐ FUEL – EAT 80% NUTRIENT DENSE FOOD THAT ENERGIZES YOU

I WAS MOST GRATEFUL FOR TODAY

Good Evening Gorgeous!

I LOVE TO GIVE. TODAY I GAVE

CHEERS TO ME!!!
LET'S CELEBRATE MY SUCCESSES FOR THE DAY

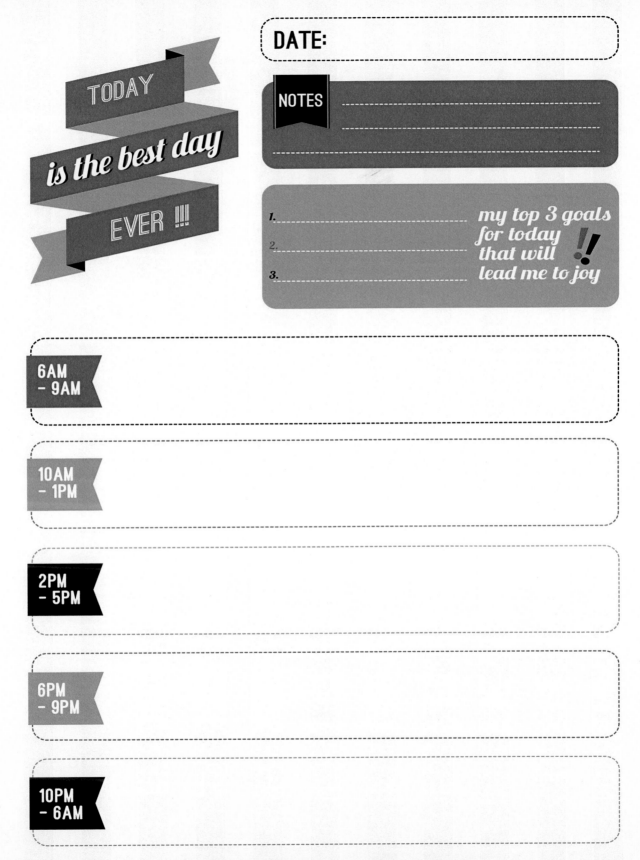

TODAY
is the best day
EVER !!!

DATE:

NOTES --

----

1. --
2. --
3. --

my top 3 goals
for today
that will
lead me to joy

6AM – 9AM

10AM – 1PM

2PM – 5PM

6PM – 9PM

10PM – 6AM

*make sure you get your sleep!

I AM BRILLIANT
gorgeous
TALENTED AND FABULOUS

GOOD MORNING *gorgeous!*

I AM GRATEFUL FOR

....
....
....

MY MANTRA

for today!

....
....
....

FUN!!! TODAY FOR FUN I WILL

☐ VISUALIZATION – SET YOUR TIMER FOR A MINIMUM OF 5 MINUTES AND GO THERE!

☐ MEDITATION – SET YOUR TIMER FOR A MINIMUM OF 5 MINUTES AND BE PRESENT, IN THE NOW. BREATHE.

☐ EXERCISE – DID YOU MOVE AT LEAST 30 MINUTES TODAY?

☐ FUEL – EAT 80% NUTRIENT DENSE FOOD THAT ENERGIZES YOU

I WAS MOST GRATEFUL FOR TODAY

Good Evening Gorgeous!

I LOVE TO GIVE. TODAY I GAVE

....
....
....

CHEERS TO ME!!!
LET'S CELEBRATE MY SUCCESSES FOR THE DAY

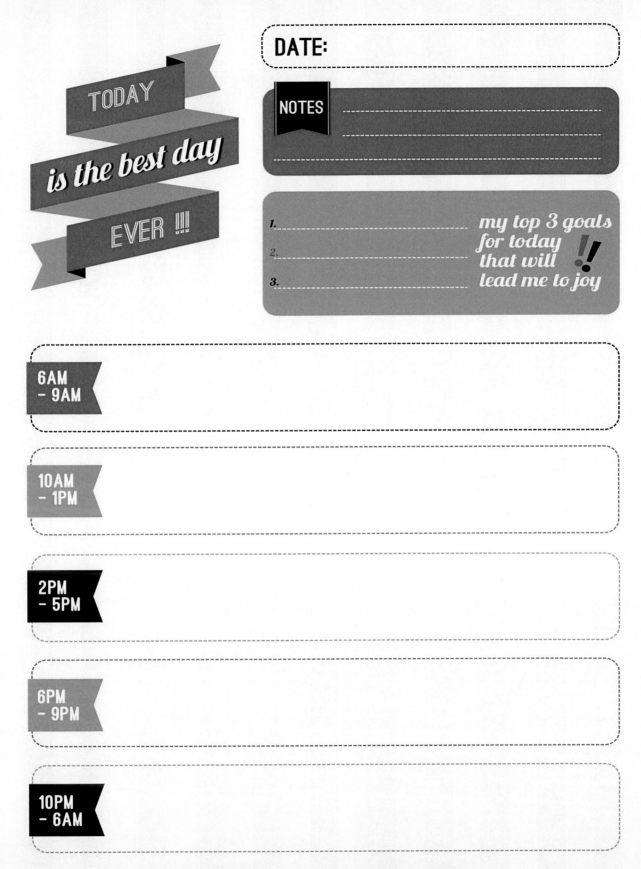

TODAY
is the best day
EVER !!!

DATE:

NOTES

1. _____
2. _____
3. _____

my top 3 goals
for today
that will
lead me to joy

6AM – 9AM

10AM – 1PM

2PM – 5PM

6PM – 9PM

10PM – 6AM

*make sure you get your sleep!

I AM BRILLIANT
gorgeous
TALENTED AND FABULOUS

GOOD MORNING *gorgeous!*

I AM GRATEFUL FOR

MY MANTRA

for today!

FUN!!! TODAY FOR FUN I WILL

☐ VISUALIZATION - SET YOUR TIMER FOR A MINIMUM OF 5 MINUTES AND GO THERE!

☐ MEDITATION - SET YOUR TIMER FOR A MINIMUM OF 5 MINUTES AND BE PRESENT, IN THE NOW. BREATHE.

☐ EXERCISE - DID YOU MOVE AT LEAST 30 MINUTES TODAY?

☐ FUEL - EAT 80% NUTRIENT DENSE FOOD THAT ENERGIZES YOU

I WAS MOST GRATEFUL FOR TODAY

Good Evening Gorgeous!

I LOVE TO GIVE.
TODAY I GAVE

CHEERS TO ME!!!
LET'S CELEBRATE MY SUCCESSES FOR THE DAY

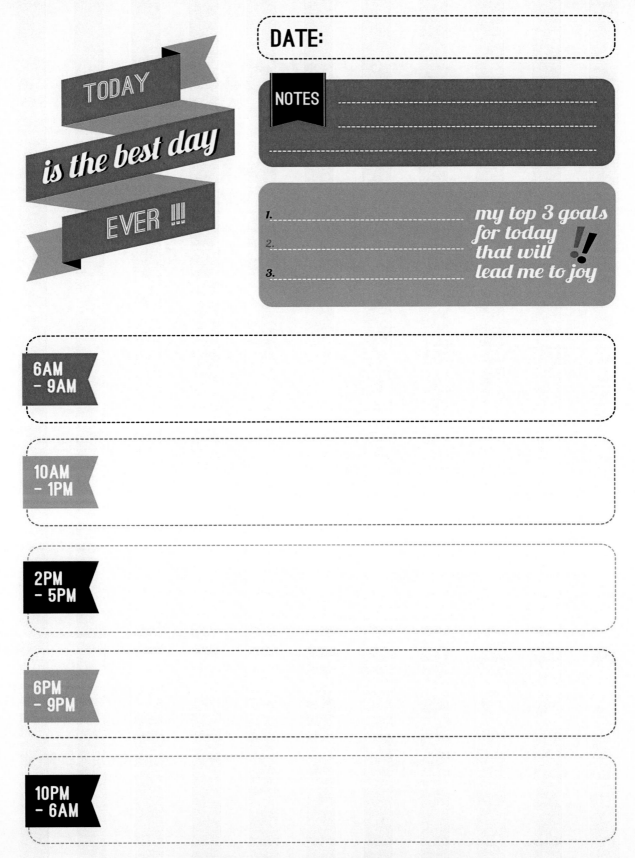

TODAY
is the best day
EVER !!!

DATE:

NOTES _____
_____
_____

1. _____
2. _____
3. _____

my top 3 goals
for today
that will !!
lead me to joy

6AM – 9AM

10AM – 1PM

2PM – 5PM

6PM – 9PM

10PM – 6AM

*make sure you get your sleep!

I AM BRILLIANT
gorgeous
TALENTED AND FABULOUS

GOOD MORNING *gorgeous!*

I AM GRATEFUL FOR

....

....

....

MY MANTRA

for today!

....

....

....

....

FUN!!! TODAY FOR FUN I WILL

....

....

....

☐ VISUALIZATION – SET YOUR TIMER FOR A MINIMUM OF 5 MINUTES AND GO THERE!

☐ MEDITATION – SET YOUR TIMER FOR A MINIMUM OF 5 MINUTES AND BE PRESENT, IN THE NOW. BREATHE.

☐ EXERCISE – DID YOU MOVE AT LEAST 30 MINUTES TODAY?

☐ FUEL – EAT 80% NUTRIENT DENSE FOOD THAT ENERGIZES YOU

I WAS MOST GRATEFUL FOR TODAY

....

....

....

....

....

....

Good Evening Gorgeous!

I LOVE TO GIVE. TODAY I GAVE

....

....

....

CHEERS TO ME!!!
LET'S CELEBRATE MY SUCCESSES FOR THE DAY

....

....

....

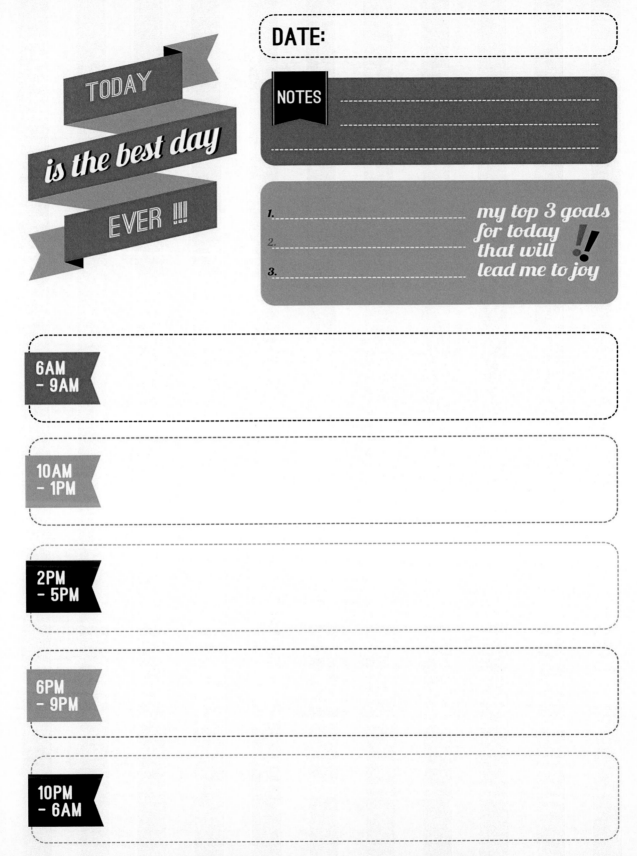

TODAY **is the best day** EVER !!!

DATE:

NOTES

1.
2.
3.

my top 3 goals for today that will lead me to joy

6AM – 9AM

10AM – 1PM

2PM – 5PM

6PM – 9PM

10PM – 6AM

make sure you get your sleep!

I AM BRILLIANT
gorgeous
TALENTED AND FABULOUS

GOOD MORNING *gorgeous!*

I AM GRATEFUL FOR

....

....

....

MY MANTRA

for today!

....

....

....

FUN!!! TODAY FOR FUN I WILL

☐ VISUALIZATION – SET YOUR TIMER FOR A MINIMUM OF 5 MINUTES AND GO THERE!

☐ MEDITATION – SET YOUR TIMER FOR A MINIMUM OF 5 MINUTES AND BE PRESENT, IN THE NOW. BREATHE.

☐ EXERCISE – DID YOU MOVE AT LEAST 30 MINUTES TODAY?

☐ FUEL – EAT 80% NUTRIENT DENSE FOOD THAT ENERGIZES YOU

I WAS MOST GRATEFUL FOR TODAY

Good Evening Gorgeous!

I LOVE TO GIVE.
TODAY I GAVE

....

....

....

CHEERS TO ME!!!
LET'S CELEBRATE MY SUCCESSES FOR THE DAY

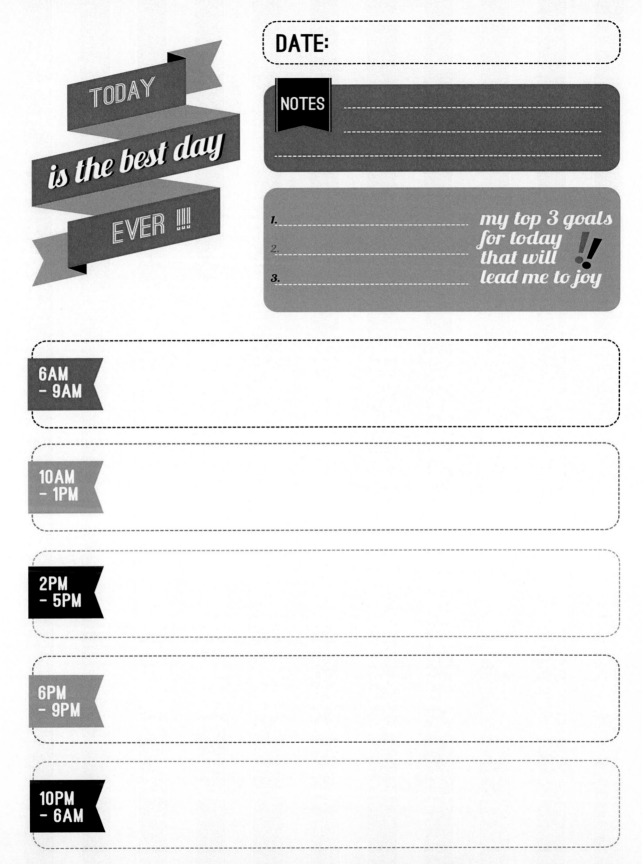

TODAY

is the best day

EVER !!!

DATE:

NOTES

1.
2.
3.

my top 3 goals
for today
that will
lead me to joy

6AM – 9AM

10AM – 1PM

2PM – 5PM

6PM – 9PM

10PM – 6AM

make sure you get your sleep!

I AM BRILLIANT
gorgeous
TALENTED AND FABULOUS

GOOD MORNING *gorgeous!*

I AM GRATEFUL FOR

MY MANTRA

for today!

FUN!!! TODAY FOR FUN I WILL

☐ VISUALIZATION – SET YOUR TIMER FOR A MINIMUM OF 5 MINUTES AND GO THERE!

☐ MEDITATION – SET YOUR TIMER FOR A MINIMUM OF 5 MINUTES AND BE PRESENT, IN THE NOW. BREATHE.

☐ EXERCISE – DID YOU MOVE AT LEAST 30 MINUTES TODAY?

☐ FUEL – EAT 80% NUTRIENT DENSE FOOD THAT ENERGIZES YOU

I WAS MOST GRATEFUL FOR TODAY

Good Evening Gorgeous!

I LOVE TO GIVE. TODAY I GAVE

CHEERS TO ME!!!
LET'S CELEBRATE MY SUCCESSES FOR THE DAY

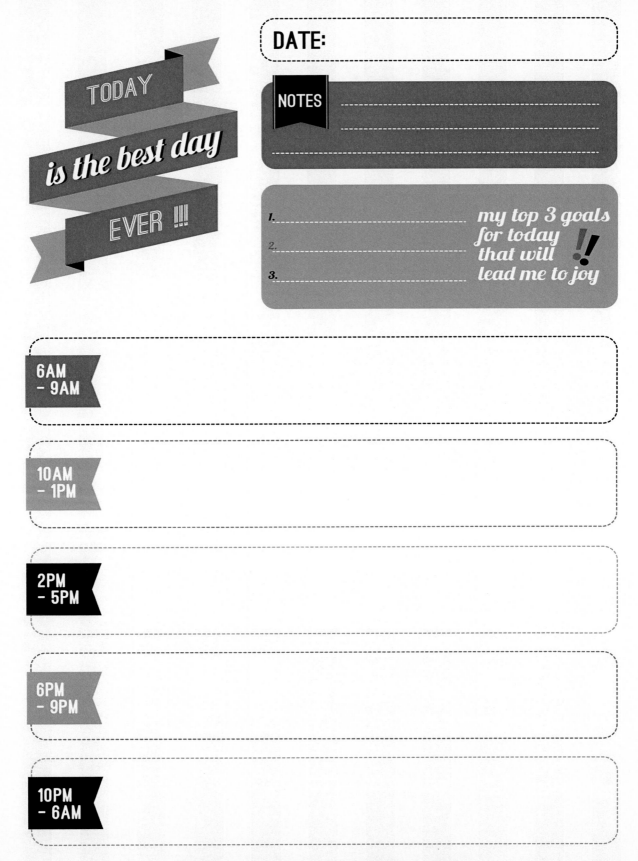

TODAY *is the best day* EVER !!!

DATE:

NOTES

1.
2.
3.

my top 3 goals for today that will lead me to joy

6AM – 9AM

10AM – 1PM

2PM – 5PM

6PM – 9PM

10PM – 6AM

make sure you get your sleep!

I AM BRILLIANT
gorgeous
TALENTED AND FABULOUS

GOOD MORNING *gorgeous!*

MY MANTRA

for today!

I AM GRATEFUL FOR

FUN!!! TODAY FOR FUN I WILL

- [ ] VISUALIZATION – SET YOUR TIMER FOR A MINIMUM OF 5 MINUTES AND GO THERE!
- [ ] MEDITATION – SET YOUR TIMER FOR A MINIMUM OF 5 MINUTES AND BE PRESENT, IN THE NOW. BREATHE.
- [ ] EXERCISE – DID YOU MOVE AT LEAST 30 MINUTES TODAY?
- [ ] FUEL – EAT 80% NUTRIENT DENSE FOOD THAT ENERGIZES YOU

Good Evening Gorgeous!

I WAS MOST GRATEFUL FOR TODAY

I LOVE TO GIVE. TODAY I GAVE

CHEERS TO ME!!!
LET'S CELEBRATE MY SUCCESSES FOR THE DAY

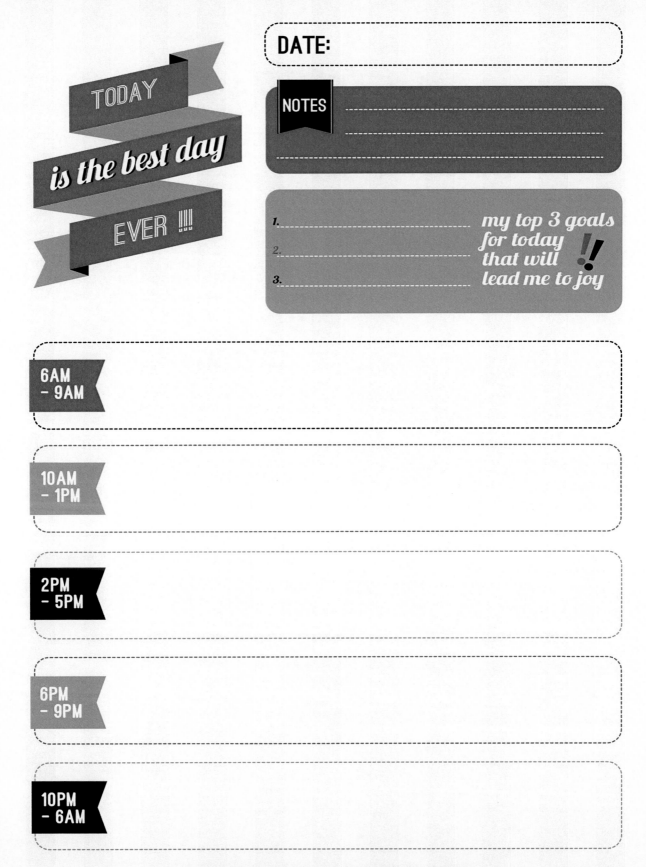

TODAY

is the best day

EVER !!!

DATE:

NOTES
....
....
....

1. ....
2. ....
3. ....

*my top 3 goals
for today
that will
lead me to joy*

6AM
– 9AM

10AM
– 1PM

2PM
– 5PM

6PM
– 9PM

10PM
– 6AM

make sure you get your sleep!

I AM BRILLIANT
gorgeous
TALENTED AND FABULOUS

GOOD MORNING *gorgeous!*

I AM GRATEFUL FOR

MY MANTRA

for today!

FUN!!! TODAY FOR FUN I WILL

- ☐ VISUALIZATION - SET YOUR TIMER FOR A MINIMUM OF 5 MINUTES AND GO THERE!
- ☐ MEDITATION - SET YOUR TIMER FOR A MINIMUM OF 5 MINUTES AND BE PRESENT, IN THE NOW. BREATHE.
- ☐ EXERCISE - DID YOU MOVE AT LEAST 30 MINUTES TODAY?
- ☐ FUEL - EAT 80% NUTRIENT DENSE FOOD THAT ENERGIZES YOU

I WAS MOST GRATEFUL FOR TODAY

Good Evening Gorgeous!

I LOVE TO GIVE. TODAY I GAVE

CHEERS TO ME!!!
LET'S CELEBRATE MY SUCCESSES FOR THE DAY

TODAY *is the best day* EVER !!!

DATE:

NOTES

1.
2.
3.

my top 3 goals for today that will lead me to joy !!

6AM – 9AM

10AM – 1PM

2PM – 5PM

6PM – 9PM

10PM – 6AM

*make sure you get your sleep!

I AM BRILLIANT
gorgeous
TALENTED AND FABULOUS

GOOD MORNING *gorgeous!*

I AM GRATEFUL FOR

....

....

....

MY MANTRA

for today!

....

....

....

....

FUN!!! TODAY FOR FUN I WILL

....

....

....

☐ VISUALIZATION – SET YOUR TIMER FOR A MINIMUM OF 5 MINUTES AND GO THERE!

☐ MEDITATION – SET YOUR TIMER FOR A MINIMUM OF 5 MINUTES AND BE PRESENT, IN THE NOW. BREATHE.

☐ EXERCISE – DID YOU MOVE AT LEAST 30 MINUTES TODAY?

☐ FUEL – EAT 80% NUTRIENT DENSE FOOD THAT ENERGIZES YOU

Good Evening Gorgeous!

I WAS MOST GRATEFUL FOR TODAY

....

....

....

....

....

....

I LOVE TO GIVE.
TODAY I GAVE

....

....

....

CHEERS TO ME!!!
LET'S CELEBRATE MY SUCCESSES FOR THE DAY

....

....

....

TODAY is the best day EVER !!!

DATE:

NOTES

1.
2.
3.

my top 3 goals
for today
that will
lead me to joy

6AM – 9AM

10AM – 1PM

2PM – 5PM

6PM – 9PM

10PM – 6AM

*make sure you get your sleep!

I AM BRILLIANT
gorgeous
TALENTED AND FABULOUS

GOOD MORNING *gorgeous!*

I AM GRATEFUL FOR

_____
_____
_____

MY MANTRA *for today!*

_____
_____
_____

FUN!!! TODAY FOR FUN I WILL

- [ ] VISUALIZATION – SET YOUR TIMER FOR A MINIMUM OF 5 MINUTES AND GO THERE!
- [ ] MEDITATION – SET YOUR TIMER FOR A MINIMUM OF 5 MINUTES AND BE PRESENT, IN THE NOW. BREATHE.
- [ ] EXERCISE – DID YOU MOVE AT LEAST 30 MINUTES TODAY?
- [ ] FUEL – EAT 80% NUTRIENT DENSE FOOD THAT ENERGIZES YOU

I WAS MOST GRATEFUL FOR TODAY

Good Evening Gorgeous!

I LOVE TO GIVE. TODAY I GAVE

_____
_____
_____

CHEERS TO ME!!!
LET'S CELEBRATE MY SUCCESSES FOR THE DAY

TODAY *is the best day* EVER !!!

DATE:

NOTES

my top 3 goals
for today
that will **!!**
lead me to joy

1.
2.
3.

6AM – 9AM

10AM – 1PM

2PM – 5PM

6PM – 9PM

10PM – 6AM

make sure you get your sleep!

I AM BRILLIANT
gorgeous
TALENTED AND FABULOUS

GOOD MORNING
gorgeous!

I AM GRATEFUL FOR

MY MANTRA

for today!

FUN!!! TODAY FOR FUN I WILL

- ☐ VISUALIZATION – SET YOUR TIMER FOR A MINIMUM OF 5 MINUTES AND GO THERE!
- ☐ MEDITATION – SET YOUR TIMER FOR A MINIMUM OF 5 MINUTES AND BE PRESENT, IN THE NOW. BREATHE.
- ☐ EXERCISE – DID YOU MOVE AT LEAST 30 MINUTES TODAY?
- ☐ FUEL – EAT 80% NUTRIENT DENSE FOOD THAT ENERGIZES YOU

I WAS MOST GRATEFUL FOR TODAY

Good Evening Gorgeous!

I LOVE TO GIVE.
TODAY I GAVE

CHEERS TO ME!!!
LET'S CELEBRATE MY SUCCESSES FOR THE DAY

TODAY

is the best day

EVER !!!

DATE:

NOTES

1.
2.
3.

*my top 3 goals
for today
that will
lead me to joy*

6AM
– 9AM

10AM
– 1PM

2PM
– 5PM

6PM
– 9PM

10PM
– 6AM

make sure you get your sleep!

I AM BRILLIANT
gorgeous
TALENTED AND FABULOUS

GOOD MORNING *gorgeous!*

I AM GRATEFUL FOR

MY MANTRA
for today!

FUN!!! TODAY FOR FUN I WILL

- ☐ VISUALIZATION – SET YOUR TIMER FOR A MINIMUM OF 5 MINUTES AND GO THERE!
- ☐ MEDITATION – SET YOUR TIMER FOR A MINIMUM OF 5 MINUTES AND BE PRESENT, IN THE NOW. BREATHE.
- ☐ EXERCISE – DID YOU MOVE AT LEAST 30 MINUTES TODAY?
- ☐ FUEL – EAT 80% NUTRIENT DENSE FOOD THAT ENERGIZES YOU

I WAS MOST GRATEFUL FOR TODAY

Good Evening Gorgeous!

I LOVE TO GIVE. TODAY I GAVE

CHEERS TO ME!!!
LET'S CELEBRATE MY SUCCESSES FOR THE DAY

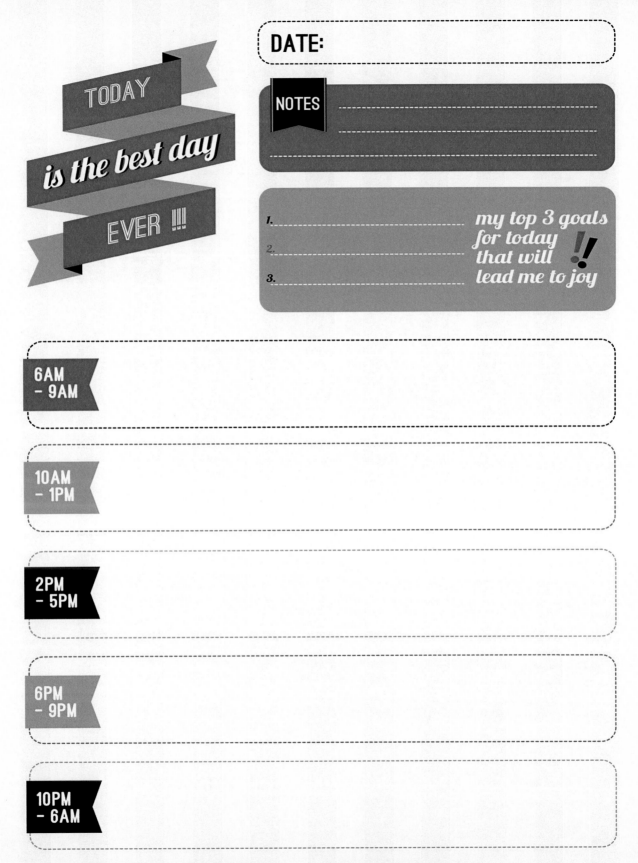

TODAY *is the best day* EVER !!!

DATE:

NOTES

1.
2.
3.

my top 3 goals for today that will lead me to joy

6AM – 9AM

10AM – 1PM

2PM – 5PM

6PM – 9PM

10PM – 6AM

make sure you get your sleep!

I AM BRILLIANT
gorgeous
TALENTED AND FABULOUS

GOOD MORNING gorgeous!

I AM GRATEFUL FOR

MY MANTRA *for today!*

FUN!!! TODAY FOR FUN I WILL

- [ ] VISUALIZATION – SET YOUR TIMER FOR A MINIMUM OF 5 MINUTES AND GO THERE!
- [ ] MEDITATION – SET YOUR TIMER FOR A MINIMUM OF 5 MINUTES AND BE PRESENT, IN THE NOW. BREATHE.
- [ ] EXERCISE – DID YOU MOVE AT LEAST 30 MINUTES TODAY?
- [ ] FUEL – EAT 80% NUTRIENT DENSE FOOD THAT ENERGIZES YOU

I WAS MOST GRATEFUL FOR TODAY

Good Evening Gorgeous!

I LOVE TO GIVE. TODAY I GAVE

CHEERS TO ME!!!
LET'S CELEBRATE MY SUCCESSES FOR THE DAY

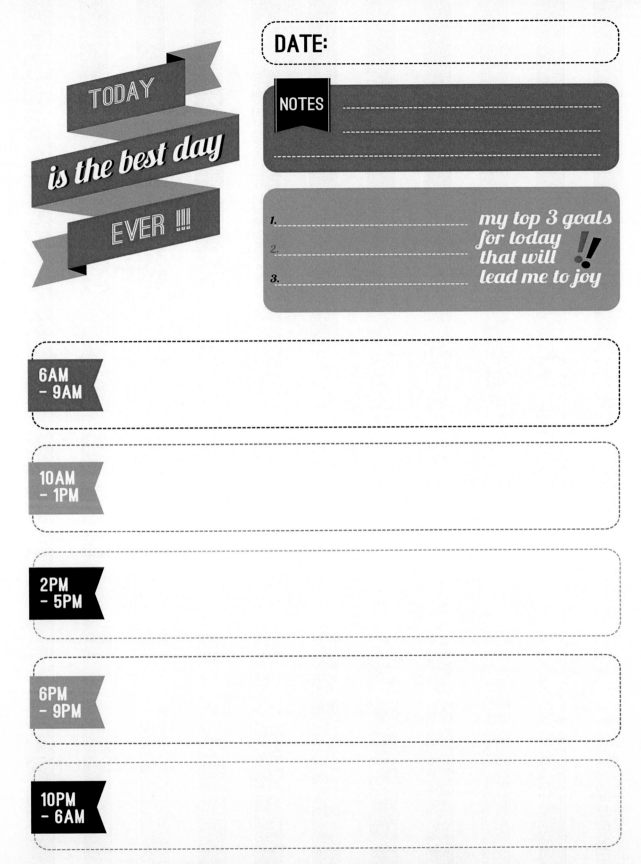

TODAY

is the best day

EVER !!!

DATE:

NOTES
- -
- -
- -

1. -
2. -
3. -

my top 3 goals for today that will lead me to joy

6AM – 9AM

10AM – 1PM

2PM – 5PM

6PM – 9PM

10PM – 6AM

make sure you get your sleep!

I AM BRILLIANT
gorgeous
TALENTED AND FABULOUS

GOOD MORNING *gorgeous!*

I AM GRATEFUL FOR

MY MANTRA *for today!*

....

....

....

FUN!!! TODAY FOR FUN I WILL

....

....

....

☐ VISUALIZATION – SET YOUR TIMER FOR A MINIMUM OF 5 MINUTES AND GO THERE!

☐ MEDITATION – SET YOUR TIMER FOR A MINIMUM OF 5 MINUTES AND BE PRESENT, IN THE NOW. BREATHE.

☐ EXERCISE – DID YOU MOVE AT LEAST 30 MINUTES TODAY?

☐ FUEL – EAT 80% NUTRIENT DENSE FOOD THAT ENERGIZES YOU

I WAS MOST GRATEFUL FOR TODAY

....

....

....

....

....

....

Good Evening Gorgeous!

I LOVE TO GIVE. TODAY I GAVE

....

....

....

CHEERS TO ME!!!
LET'S CELEBRATE MY SUCCESSES FOR THE DAY

....

....

....

....

TODAY *is the best day* EVER !!!

DATE:

NOTES
- -
- -
- -

1. -
2. -
3. -

my top 3 goals for today that will lead me to joy

6AM – 9AM

10AM – 1PM

2PM – 5PM

6PM – 9PM

10PM – 6AM

make sure you get your sleep!

I AM BRILLIANT
gorgeous
TALENTED AND FABULOUS

GOOD MORNING *gorgeous!*

I AM GRATEFUL FOR

MY MANTRA

for today!

FUN!!! TODAY FOR FUN I WILL

- [ ] VISUALIZATION – SET YOUR TIMER FOR A MINIMUM OF 5 MINUTES AND GO THERE!
- [ ] MEDITATION – SET YOUR TIMER FOR A MINIMUM OF 5 MINUTES AND BE PRESENT, IN THE NOW. BREATHE.
- [ ] EXERCISE – DID YOU MOVE AT LEAST 30 MINUTES TODAY?
- [ ] FUEL – EAT 80% NUTRIENT DENSE FOOD THAT ENERGIZES YOU

I WAS MOST GRATEFUL FOR TODAY

Good Evening Gorgeous!

I LOVE TO GIVE. TODAY I GAVE

CHEERS TO ME!!!
LET'S CELEBRATE MY SUCCESSES FOR THE DAY

TODAY *is the best day* EVER !!!

DATE:

NOTES

1.
2.
3.

my top 3 goals for today that will lead me to joy

6AM – 9AM

10AM – 1PM

2PM – 5PM

6PM – 9PM

10PM – 6AM

make sure you get your sleep!

I AM BRILLIANT
gorgeous
TALENTED AND FABULOUS

GOOD MORNING *gorgeous!*

I AM GRATEFUL FOR

MY MANTRA

for today!

FUN!!! TODAY FOR FUN I WILL

- ☐ VISUALIZATION - SET YOUR TIMER FOR A MINIMUM OF 5 MINUTES AND GO THERE!
- ☐ MEDITATION - SET YOUR TIMER FOR A MINIMUM OF 5 MINUTES AND BE PRESENT, IN THE NOW. BREATHE.
- ☐ EXERCISE - DID YOU MOVE AT LEAST 30 MINUTES TODAY?
- ☐ FUEL - EAT 80% NUTRIENT DENSE FOOD THAT ENERGIZES YOU

I WAS MOST GRATEFUL FOR TODAY

Good Evening Gorgeous!

I LOVE TO GIVE.
TODAY I GAVE

CHEERS TO ME!!!
LET'S CELEBRATE MY SUCCESSES FOR THE DAY

DATE:

NOTES

1.
2.
3.

my top 3 goals for today that will lead me to joy

6AM – 9AM

10AM – 1PM

2PM – 5PM

6PM – 9PM

10PM – 6AM

make sure you get your sleep!

PAUSE CAFÉ

coffee break **;;**

time to pause and reflect. are you focused on your goals? need to revise your priorities? get more specific with your visualization? add some new mantras? grab a cup of hot coffee or tea and sit down and focus on your joyful plan for the next 30 days.

L'ART DE VIVRE!

VISUALIZE THE NEXT 30 DAYS

RAISON D'ÊTRE!

WHAT ARE YOUR TOP 2-3 PRIORITIES?

PAIN AU CHOCOLAT

FOR YOUR BRAIN!

MANTRAS AND AFFIRMATIONS YOU NEED TO HEAR DAILY

LA VIE EST BELLE!

WHAT ARE YOU MOST GRATEFUL FOR FROM THE LAST 30 DAYS?

VIVRE LA VIE PAR LA CONCEPTION!

REVISIT YOUR 10 GOALS FOR THE YEAR

(THINGS CHANGE, PERSPECTIVE, PRIORITIES OR MAYBE YOU ACCOMPLISHED A GOAL AND WOULD LIKE TO ADD ANOTHER. OR, MAYBE THEY ARE THE SAME AND YOU NEED TO REWRITE THEM HERE)

I AM BRILLIANT
gorgeous
TALENTED AND FABULOUS

GOOD MORNING *gorgeous!*

I AM GRATEFUL FOR

_____
_____
_____
_____

MY MANTRA *for today!*

_____
_____
_____

FUN!!! TODAY FOR FUN I WILL

_____
_____
_____

☐ VISUALIZATION – SET YOUR TIMER FOR A MINIMUM OF 5 MINUTES AND GO THERE!

☐ MEDITATION – SET YOUR TIMER FOR A MINIMUM OF 5 MINUTES AND BE PRESENT, IN THE NOW. BREATHE.

☐ EXERCISE – DID YOU MOVE AT LEAST 30 MINUTES TODAY?

☐ FUEL – EAT 80% NUTRIENT DENSE FOOD THAT ENERGIZES YOU

I WAS MOST GRATEFUL FOR TODAY

_____
_____
_____
_____
_____
_____

Good Evening Gorgeous!

I LOVE TO GIVE. TODAY I GAVE

_____
_____
_____

CHEERS TO ME!!!
LET'S CELEBRATE MY SUCCESSES FOR THE DAY

_____
_____
_____
_____

TODAY *is the best day* **EVER !!!**

DATE:

NOTES ....
....
....

1. ....
2. ....
3. ....

my top 3 goals for today that will lead me to joy

6AM – 9AM

10AM – 1PM

2PM – 5PM

6PM – 9PM

10PM – 6AM

make sure you get your sleep!

I AM BRILLIANT
gorgeous
TALENTED AND FABULOUS

GOOD MORNING *gorgeous!*

I AM GRATEFUL FOR

MY MANTRA

for today!

FUN!!! TODAY FOR FUN I WILL

☐ VISUALIZATION – SET YOUR TIMER FOR A MINIMUM OF 5 MINUTES AND GO THERE!

☐ MEDITATION – SET YOUR TIMER FOR A MINIMUM OF 5 MINUTES AND BE PRESENT, IN THE NOW. BREATHE.

☐ EXERCISE – DID YOU MOVE AT LEAST 30 MINUTES TODAY?

☐ FUEL – EAT 80% NUTRIENT DENSE FOOD THAT ENERGIZES YOU

Good Evening Gorgeous!

I WAS MOST GRATEFUL FOR TODAY

I LOVE TO GIVE.
TODAY I GAVE

CHEERS TO ME!!!
LET'S CELEBRATE MY SUCCESSES FOR THE DAY

TODAY
is the best day
EVER !!!!

DATE:

NOTES

1.
2.
3.

*my top 3 goals
for today
that will
lead me to joy*

6AM – 9AM

10AM – 1PM

2PM – 5PM

6PM – 9PM

10PM – 6AM

make sure you get your sleep!

I AM BRILLIANT
gorgeous
TALENTED AND FABULOUS

GOOD MORNING *gorgeous!*

I AM GRATEFUL FOR

MY MANTRA

for today!

FUN!!! TODAY FOR FUN I WILL

- VISUALIZATION – SET YOUR TIMER FOR A MINIMUM OF 5 MINUTES AND GO THERE!
- MEDITATION – SET YOUR TIMER FOR A MINIMUM OF 5 MINUTES AND BE PRESENT, IN THE NOW. BREATHE.
- EXERCISE – DID YOU MOVE AT LEAST 30 MINUTES TODAY?
- FUEL – EAT 80% NUTRIENT DENSE FOOD THAT ENERGIZES YOU

I WAS MOST GRATEFUL FOR TODAY

Good Evening Gorgeous!

I LOVE TO GIVE. TODAY I GAVE

CHEERS TO ME!!!
LET'S CELEBRATE MY SUCCESSES FOR THE DAY

TODAY *is the best day* EVER !!!

DATE:

NOTES --

----

1. ---
2. ---
3. ---

my top 3 goals for today that will lead me to joy

6AM – 9AM

10AM – 1PM

2PM – 5PM

6PM – 9PM

10PM – 6AM

make sure you get your sleep!

I AM BRILLIANT
gorgeous
TALENTED AND FABULOUS

GOOD MORNING *gorgeous!*

I AM GRATEFUL FOR

MY MANTRA

for today!

FUN!!! TODAY FOR FUN I WILL

☐ VISUALIZATION – SET YOUR TIMER FOR A MINIMUM OF 5 MINUTES AND GO THERE!

☐ MEDITATION – SET YOUR TIMER FOR A MINIMUM OF 5 MINUTES AND BE PRESENT, IN THE NOW. BREATHE.

☐ EXERCISE – DID YOU MOVE AT LEAST 30 MINUTES TODAY?

☐ FUEL – EAT 80% NUTRIENT DENSE FOOD THAT ENERGIZES YOU

I WAS MOST GRATEFUL FOR TODAY

Good Evening Gorgeous!

I LOVE TO GIVE. TODAY I GAVE

CHEERS TO ME!!!
LET'S CELEBRATE MY SUCCESSES FOR THE DAY

TODAY

is the best day

EVER !!!

DATE:

NOTES

----

1. --
2. --
3. --

my top 3 goals
for today
that will
lead me to joy

6AM
– 9AM

10AM
– 1PM

2PM
– 5PM

6PM
– 9PM

10PM
– 6AM

*make sure you get your sleep!

I AM BRILLIANT
gorgeous
TALENTED AND FABULOUS

GOOD MORNING *gorgeous!*

I AM GRATEFUL FOR

MY MANTRA *for today!*

FUN!!! TODAY FOR FUN I WILL

- [ ] VISUALIZATION - SET YOUR TIMER FOR A MINIMUM OF 5 MINUTES AND GO THERE!
- [ ] MEDITATION - SET YOUR TIMER FOR A MINIMUM OF 5 MINUTES AND BE PRESENT, IN THE NOW, BREATHE.
- [ ] EXERCISE - DID YOU MOVE AT LEAST 30 MINUTES TODAY?
- [ ] FUEL - EAT 80% NUTRIENT DENSE FOOD THAT ENERGIZES YOU

I WAS MOST GRATEFUL FOR TODAY

Good Evening Gorgeous!

I LOVE TO GIVE. TODAY I GAVE

CHEERS TO ME!!!
LET'S CELEBRATE MY SUCCESSES FOR THE DAY

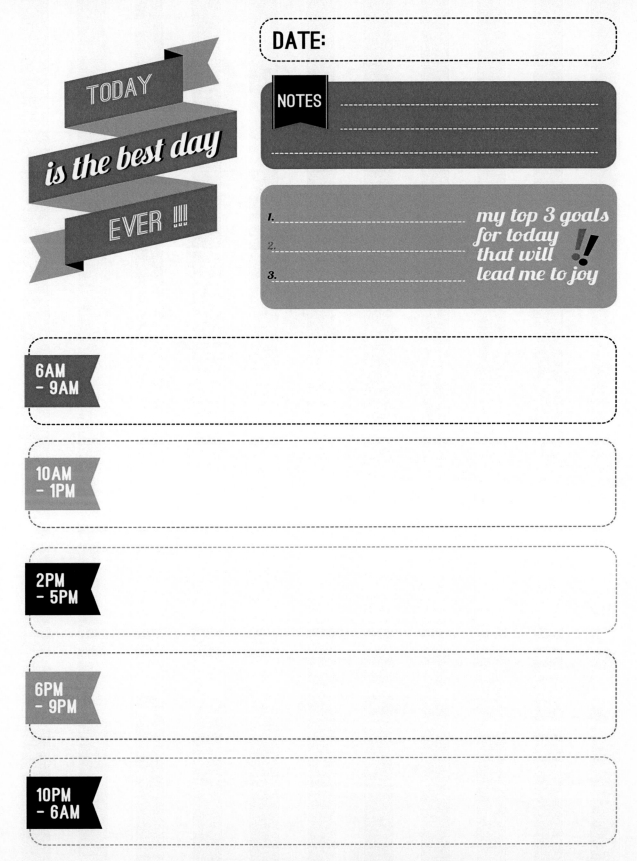

DATE:

NOTES

1. ....
2. ....
3. ....

my top 3 goals
for today
that will
lead me to joy

6AM
- 9AM

10AM
- 1PM

2PM
- 5PM

6PM
- 9PM

10PM
- 6AM

TODAY
is the best day
EVER !!!

make sure you get your sleep!

I AM BRILLIANT
gorgeous
TALENTED AND FABULOUS

GOOD MORNING *gorgeous!*

I AM GRATEFUL FOR

MY MANTRA

for today!

FUN!!! TODAY FOR FUN I WILL

☐ VISUALIZATION – SET YOUR TIMER FOR A MINIMUM OF 5 MINUTES AND GO THERE!

☐ MEDITATION – SET YOUR TIMER FOR A MINIMUM OF 5 MINUTES AND BE PRESENT, IN THE NOW. BREATHE.

☐ EXERCISE – DID YOU MOVE AT LEAST 30 MINUTES TODAY?

☐ FUEL – EAT 80% NUTRIENT DENSE FOOD THAT ENERGIZES YOU

I WAS MOST GRATEFUL FOR TODAY

Good Evening Gorgeous!

I LOVE TO GIVE.
TODAY I GAVE

CHEERS TO ME!!!
LET'S CELEBRATE MY SUCCESSES FOR THE DAY

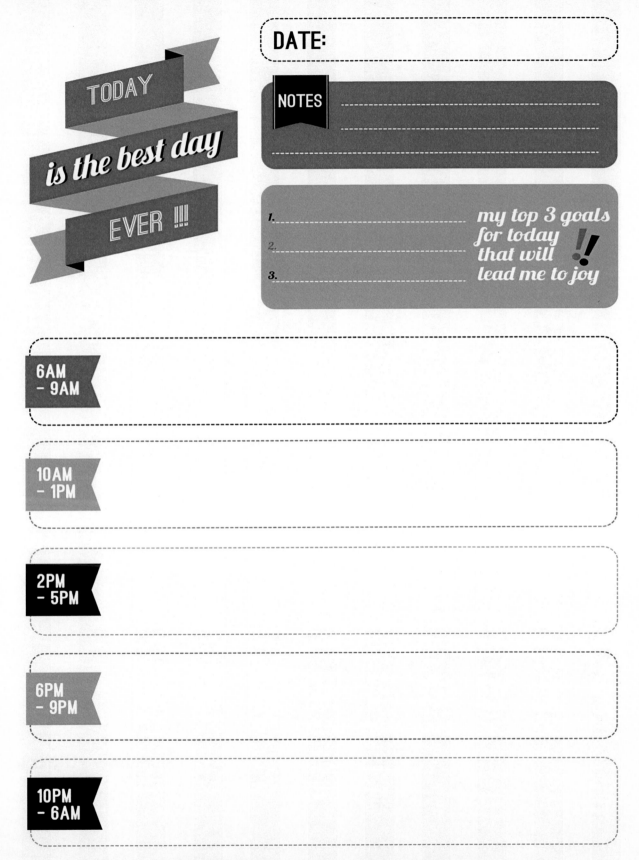

TODAY

is the best day

EVER !!!

DATE:

NOTES

----

1. --
2. --
3. --

my top 3 goals for today that will lead me to joy

6AM – 9AM

10AM – 1PM

2PM – 5PM

6PM – 9PM

10PM – 6AM

make sure you get your sleep!

I AM BRILLIANT
gorgeous
TALENTED AND FABULOUS

GOOD MORNING *gorgeous!*

MY MANTRA

for today!

I AM GRATEFUL FOR

FUN!!! TODAY FOR FUN I WILL

- [ ] VISUALIZATION – SET YOUR TIMER FOR A MINIMUM OF 5 MINUTES AND GO THERE!
- [ ] MEDITATION – SET YOUR TIMER FOR A MINIMUM OF 5 MINUTES AND BE PRESENT, IN THE NOW. BREATHE.
- [ ] EXERCISE – DID YOU MOVE AT LEAST 30 MINUTES TODAY?
- [ ] FUEL – EAT 80% NUTRIENT DENSE FOOD THAT ENERGIZES YOU

I WAS MOST GRATEFUL FOR TODAY

Good Evening Gorgeous!

I LOVE TO GIVE. TODAY I GAVE

CHEERS TO ME!!!
LET'S CELEBRATE MY SUCCESSES FOR THE DAY

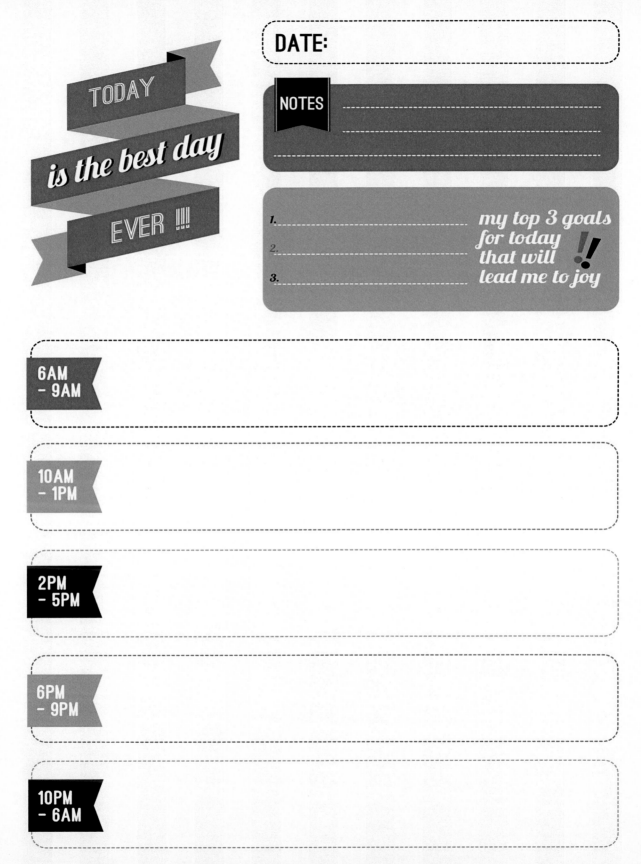

TODAY *is the best day* **EVER !!!**

DATE:

NOTES
_____
_____
_____

1. _____
2. _____
3. _____

my top 3 goals for today that will lead me to joy

6AM – 9AM

10AM – 1PM

2PM – 5PM

6PM – 9PM

10PM – 6AM

make sure you get your sleep!

I AM BRILLIANT
gorgeous
TALENTED AND FABULOUS

GOOD MORNING
gorgeous!

I AM GRATEFUL FOR

MY MANTRA

for today!

FUN!!! TODAY FOR FUN I WILL

☐ VISUALIZATION – SET YOUR TIMER FOR A MINIMUM OF 5 MINUTES AND GO THERE!

☐ MEDITATION – SET YOUR TIMER FOR A MINIMUM OF 5 MINUTES AND BE PRESENT, IN THE NOW. BREATHE.

☐ EXERCISE – DID YOU MOVE AT LEAST 30 MINUTES TODAY?

☐ FUEL – EAT 80% NUTRIENT DENSE FOOD THAT ENERGIZES YOU

Good Evening Gorgeous!

I WAS MOST GRATEFUL FOR TODAY

I LOVE TO GIVE.
TODAY I GAVE

CHEERS TO ME!!!
LET'S CELEBRATE MY SUCCESSES FOR THE DAY

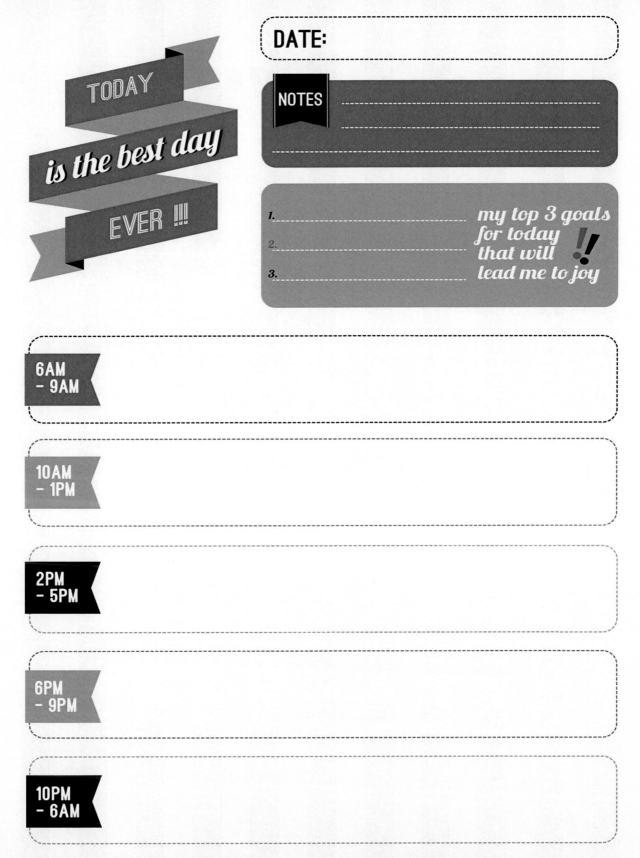

TODAY
is the best day
EVER !!!

DATE:

NOTES

1.
2.
3.
my top 3 goals for today that will lead me to joy

6AM – 9AM

10AM – 1PM

2PM – 5PM

6PM – 9PM

10PM – 6AM

make sure you get your sleep!

I AM BRILLIANT
gorgeous
TALENTED AND FABULOUS

GOOD MORNING *gorgeous!*

I AM GRATEFUL FOR

MY MANTRA

for today!

FUN!!! TODAY FOR FUN I WILL

- [ ] **VISUALIZATION** – SET YOUR TIMER FOR A MINIMUM OF 5 MINUTES AND GO THERE!
- [ ] **MEDITATION** – SET YOUR TIMER FOR A MINIMUM OF 5 MINUTES AND BE PRESENT, IN THE NOW. BREATHE.
- [ ] **EXERCISE** – DID YOU MOVE AT LEAST 30 MINUTES TODAY?
- [ ] **FUEL** – EAT 80% NUTRIENT DENSE FOOD THAT ENERGIZES YOU

I WAS MOST GRATEFUL FOR TODAY

Good Evening Gorgeous!

I LOVE TO GIVE. TODAY I GAVE

CHEERS TO ME!!!
LET'S CELEBRATE MY SUCCESSES FOR THE DAY

TODAY
is the best day
EVER !!!

DATE:

NOTES

1.
2.
3.

*my top 3 goals
for today
that will
lead me to joy* !!

6AM – 9AM

10AM – 1PM

2PM – 5PM

6PM – 9PM

10PM – 6AM

make sure you get your sleep!

I AM BRILLIANT
gorgeous
TALENTED AND FABULOUS

GOOD MORNING *gorgeous!*

I AM GRATEFUL FOR

MY MANTRA *for today!*

FUN!!! TODAY FOR FUN I WILL

- ☐ VISUALIZATION – SET YOUR TIMER FOR A MINIMUM OF 5 MINUTES AND GO THERE!
- ☐ MEDITATION – SET YOUR TIMER FOR A MINIMUM OF 5 MINUTES AND BE PRESENT, IN THE NOW. BREATHE.
- ☐ EXERCISE – DID YOU MOVE AT LEAST 30 MINUTES TODAY?
- ☐ FUEL – EAT 80% NUTRIENT DENSE FOOD THAT ENERGIZES YOU

I WAS MOST GRATEFUL FOR TODAY

Good Evening Gorgeous!

I LOVE TO GIVE. TODAY I GAVE

CHEERS TO ME!!!
LET'S CELEBRATE MY SUCCESSES FOR THE DAY

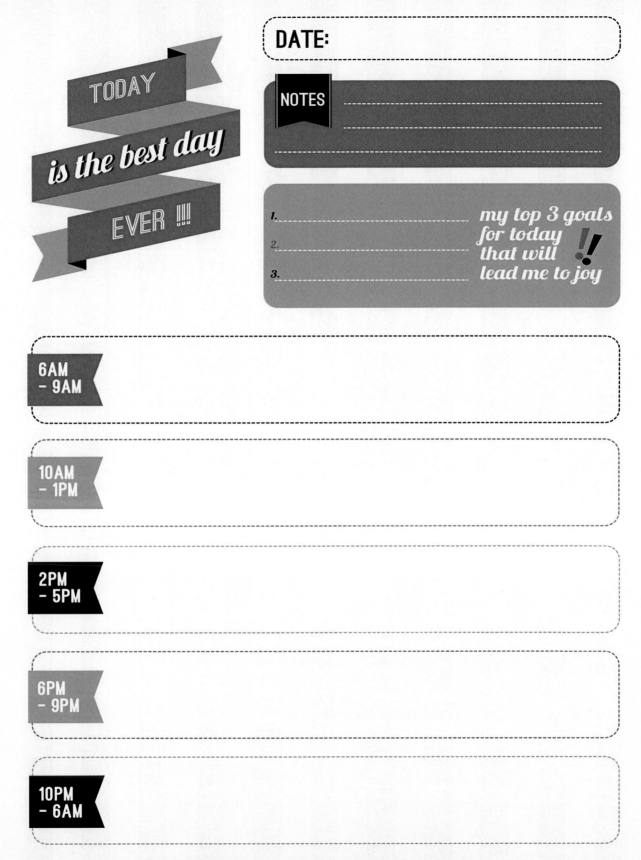

TODAY
is the best day
EVER !!!

DATE:

NOTES

1.
2.
3.

my top 3 goals for today that will lead me to joy

6AM – 9AM

10AM – 1PM

2PM – 5PM

6PM – 9PM

10PM – 6AM

make sure you get your sleep!

I AM BRILLIANT
gorgeous
TALENTED AND FABULOUS

GOOD MORNING *gorgeous!*

I AM GRATEFUL FOR

MY MANTRA

for today!

FUN!!! TODAY FOR FUN I WILL

- [ ] VISUALIZATION - SET YOUR TIMER FOR A MINIMUM OF 5 MINUTES AND GO THERE!
- [ ] MEDITATION - SET YOUR TIMER FOR A MINIMUM OF 5 MINUTES AND BE PRESENT, IN THE NOW. BREATHE.
- [ ] EXERCISE - DID YOU MOVE AT LEAST 30 MINUTES TODAY?
- [ ] FUEL - EAT 80% NUTRIENT DENSE FOOD THAT ENERGIZES YOU

I WAS MOST GRATEFUL FOR TODAY

Good Evening Gorgeous!

I LOVE TO GIVE. TODAY I GAVE

CHEERS TO ME!!!
LET'S CELEBRATE MY SUCCESSES FOR THE DAY

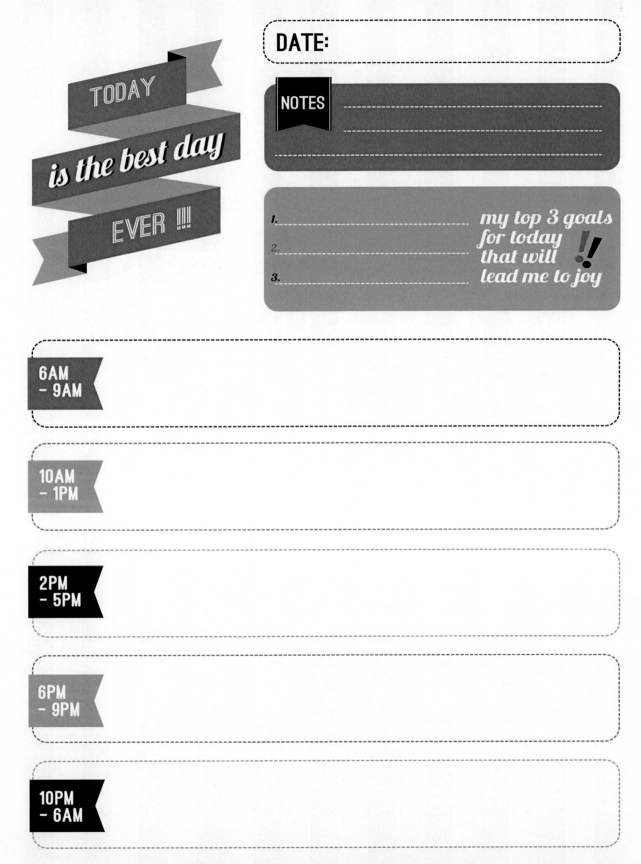

TODAY
is the best day
EVER !!!

DATE:

NOTES

1.
2.
3.

*my top 3 goals
for today
that will
lead me to joy*

6AM – 9AM

10AM – 1PM

2PM – 5PM

6PM – 9PM

10PM – 6AM

make sure you get your sleep!

I AM BRILLIANT
gorgeous
TALENTED AND FABULOUS

GOOD MORNING
gorgeous!

I AM GRATEFUL FOR

MY MANTRA

for today!

FUN!!! TODAY FOR FUN I WILL

☐ VISUALIZATION – SET YOUR TIMER FOR A MINIMUM OF 5 MINUTES AND GO THERE!

☐ MEDITATION – SET YOUR TIMER FOR A MINIMUM OF 5 MINUTES AND BE PRESENT, IN THE NOW. BREATHE.

☐ EXERCISE – DID YOU MOVE AT LEAST 30 MINUTES TODAY?

☐ FUEL – EAT 80% NUTRIENT DENSE FOOD THAT ENERGIZES YOU

I WAS MOST GRATEFUL FOR TODAY

Good Evening Gorgeous!

I LOVE TO GIVE.
TODAY I GAVE

CHEERS TO ME!!!
LET'S CELEBRATE MY SUCCESSES FOR THE DAY

TODAY *is the best day* **EVER !!!**

DATE:

NOTES

1.
2.
3.

my top 3 goals for today that will lead me to joy **!!**

6AM – 9AM

10AM – 1PM

2PM – 5PM

6PM – 9PM

10PM – 6AM

make sure you get your sleep!

I AM BRILLIANT
gorgeous
TALENTED AND FABULOUS

GOOD MORNING *gorgeous!*

I AM GRATEFUL FOR

....

....

....

MY MANTRA

for today!

....

....

....

....

FUN!!! TODAY FOR FUN I WILL

....

....

....

☐ VISUALIZATION – SET YOUR TIMER FOR A MINIMUM OF 5 MINUTES AND GO THERE!

☐ MEDITATION – SET YOUR TIMER FOR A MINIMUM OF 5 MINUTES AND BE PRESENT, IN THE NOW. BREATHE.

☐ EXERCISE – DID YOU MOVE AT LEAST 30 MINUTES TODAY?

☐ FUEL – EAT 80% NUTRIENT DENSE FOOD THAT ENERGIZES YOU

I WAS MOST GRATEFUL FOR TODAY

....

....

....

....

....

....

Good Evening Gorgeous!

I LOVE TO GIVE.
TODAY I GAVE

....

....

....

CHEERS TO ME!!!
LET'S CELEBRATE MY SUCCESSES FOR THE DAY

....

....

....

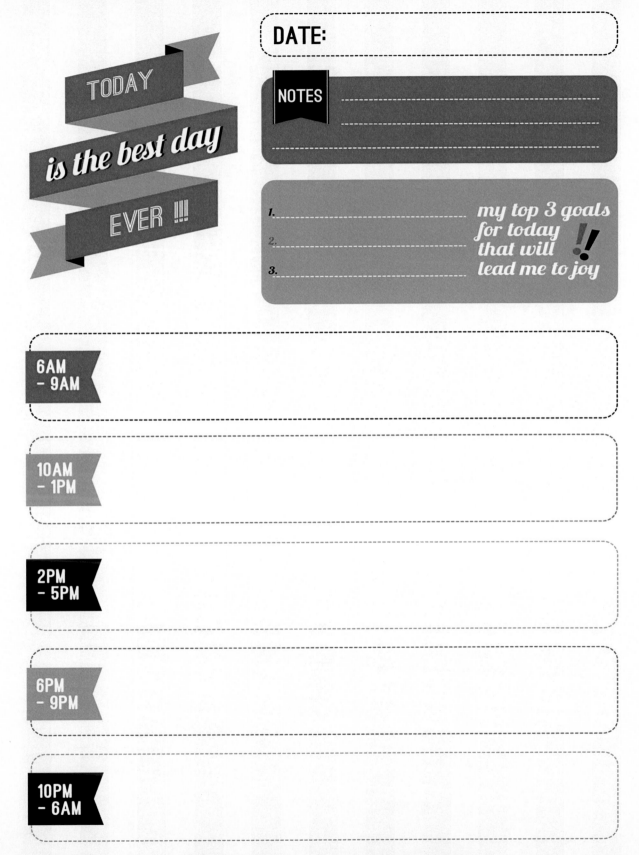

TODAY *is the best day* EVER !!!

DATE:

NOTES _____
_____
_____

1. _____
2. _____
3. _____

my top 3 goals for today that will lead me to joy

6AM – 9AM

10AM – 1PM

2PM – 5PM

6PM – 9PM

10PM – 6AM

make sure you get your sleep!

I AM BRILLIANT
gorgeous
TALENTED AND FABULOUS

GOOD MORNING *gorgeous!*

MY MANTRA *for today!*

_____
_____
_____
_____

I AM GRATEFUL FOR

_____
_____
_____
_____

FUN!!! TODAY FOR FUN I WILL

_____
_____
_____

- [ ] VISUALIZATION – SET YOUR TIMER FOR A MINIMUM OF 5 MINUTES AND GO THERE!
- [ ] MEDITATION – SET YOUR TIMER FOR A MINIMUM OF 5 MINUTES AND BE PRESENT, IN THE NOW. BREATHE.
- [ ] EXERCISE – DID YOU MOVE AT LEAST 30 MINUTES TODAY?
- [ ] FUEL – EAT 80% NUTRIENT DENSE FOOD THAT ENERGIZES YOU

I WAS MOST GRATEFUL FOR TODAY

_____
_____
_____
_____
_____
_____
_____

Good Evening Gorgeous!

I LOVE TO GIVE. TODAY I GAVE

_____
_____
_____

CHEERS TO ME!!!
LET'S CELEBRATE MY SUCCESSES FOR THE DAY

_____
_____
_____

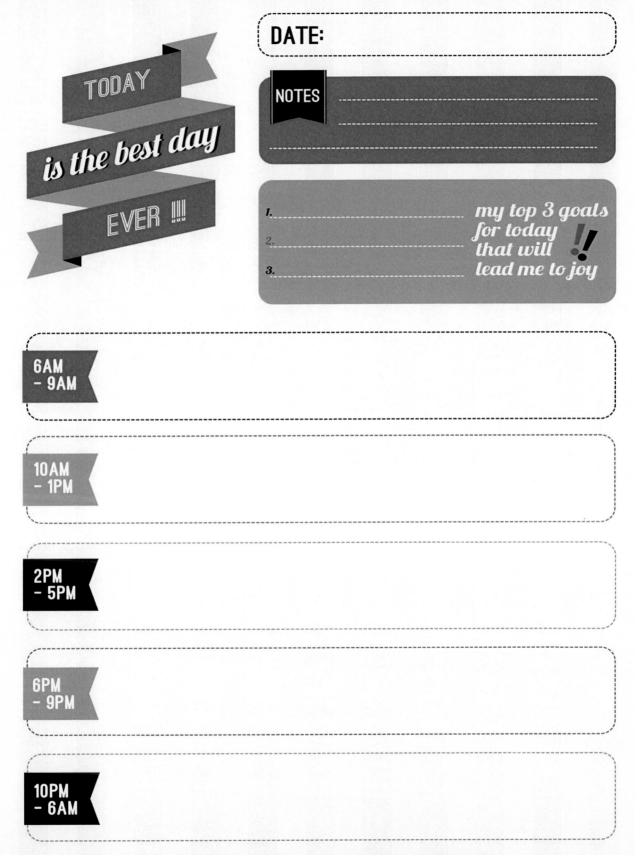

TODAY

is the best day

EVER !!!

DATE:

NOTES

1.
2.
3.

my top 3 goals for today that will lead me to joy

6AM – 9AM

10AM – 1PM

2PM – 5PM

6PM – 9PM

10PM – 6AM

make sure you get your sleep!

I AM BRILLIANT
gorgeous
TALENTED AND FABULOUS

GOOD MORNING *gorgeous!*

I AM GRATEFUL FOR

_____

_____

_____

MY MANTRA

for today!

_____

_____

_____

_____

FUN!!! TODAY FOR FUN I WILL

_____

_____

_____

- ☐ VISUALIZATION – SET YOUR TIMER FOR A MINIMUM OF 5 MINUTES AND GO THERE!
- ☐ MEDITATION – SET YOUR TIMER FOR A MINIMUM OF 5 MINUTES AND BE PRESENT, IN THE NOW. BREATHE.
- ☐ EXERCISE – DID YOU MOVE AT LEAST 30 MINUTES TODAY?
- ☐ FUEL – EAT 80% NUTRIENT DENSE FOOD THAT ENERGIZES YOU

I WAS MOST GRATEFUL FOR TODAY

_____

_____

_____

_____

_____

Good Evening Gorgeous!

I LOVE TO GIVE. TODAY I GAVE

_____

_____

_____

CHEERS TO ME!!!
LET'S CELEBRATE MY SUCCESSES FOR THE DAY

_____

_____

_____

_____

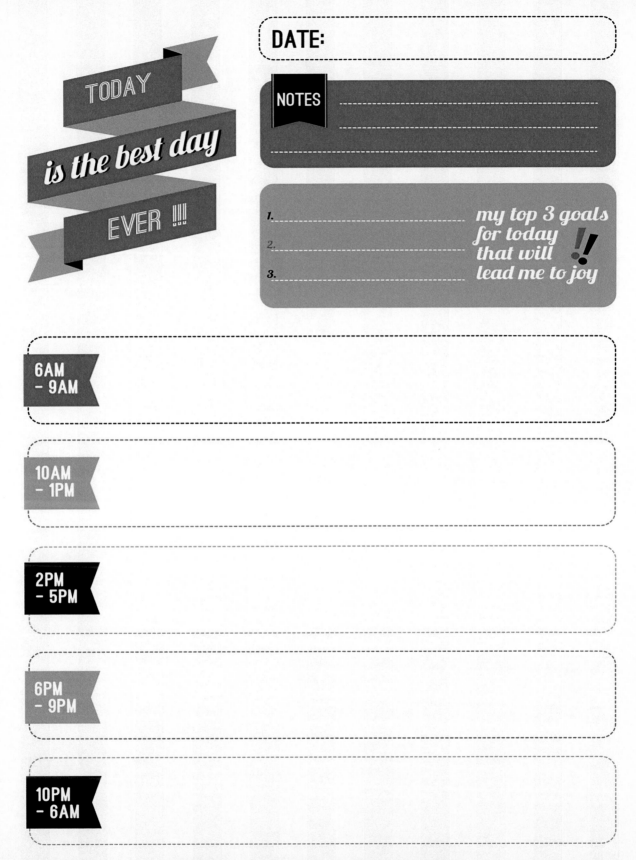

TODAY *is the best day* **EVER !!!!**

DATE:

NOTES

my top 3 goals for today that will lead me to joy !!

1.
2.
3.

6AM – 9AM

10AM – 1PM

2PM – 5PM

6PM – 9PM

10PM – 6AM

make sure you get your sleep!

I AM BRILLIANT
gorgeous
TALENTED AND FABULOUS

GOOD MORNING *gorgeous!*

I AM GRATEFUL FOR

....
....
....

MY MANTRA

for today!

....
....
....
....

FUN!!! TODAY FOR FUN I WILL

☐ VISUALIZATION - SET YOUR TIMER FOR A MINIMUM OF 5 MINUTES AND GO THERE!

☐ MEDITATION - SET YOUR TIMER FOR A MINIMUM OF 5 MINUTES AND BE PRESENT, IN THE NOW. BREATHE.

☐ EXERCISE - DID YOU MOVE AT LEAST 30 MINUTES TODAY?

☐ FUEL - EAT 80% NUTRIENT DENSE FOOD THAT ENERGIZES YOU

I WAS MOST GRATEFUL FOR TODAY

Good Evening Gorgeous!

I LOVE TO GIVE. TODAY I GAVE

....
....
....

CHEERS TO ME!!!
LET'S CELEBRATE MY SUCCESSES FOR THE DAY

TODAY is the best day EVER !!!

DATE:

NOTES

1.
2.
3.

my top 3 goals
for today
that will
lead me to joy

6AM – 9AM

10AM – 1PM

2PM – 5PM

6PM – 9PM

10PM – 6AM

*make sure you get your sleep!

I AM BRILLIANT
gorgeous
TALENTED AND FABULOUS

GOOD MORNING *gorgeous!*

I AM GRATEFUL FOR

MY MANTRA

for today!

FUN!!! TODAY FOR FUN I WILL

☐ VISUALIZATION – SET YOUR TIMER FOR A MINIMUM OF 5 MINUTES AND GO THERE!

☐ MEDITATION – SET YOUR TIMER FOR A MINIMUM OF 5 MINUTES AND BE PRESENT, IN THE NOW. BREATHE.

☐ EXERCISE – DID YOU MOVE AT LEAST 30 MINUTES TODAY?

☐ FUEL – EAT 80% NUTRIENT DENSE FOOD THAT ENERGIZES YOU

I WAS MOST GRATEFUL FOR TODAY

Good Evening Gorgeous!

I LOVE TO GIVE. TODAY I GAVE

CHEERS TO ME!!!
LET'S CELEBRATE MY SUCCESSES FOR THE DAY

TODAY

is the best day

EVER !!!

DATE:

NOTES

1.
2.
3.

my top 3 goals
for today
that will
lead me to joy !!

6AM
- 9AM

10AM
- 1PM

2PM
- 5PM

6PM
- 9PM

10PM
- 6AM

make sure you get your sleep!

I AM BRILLIANT
gorgeous
TALENTED AND FABULOUS

GOOD MORNING *gorgeous!*

I AM GRATEFUL FOR

MY MANTRA

for today!

FUN!!! TODAY FOR FUN I WILL

- [ ] VISUALIZATION – SET YOUR TIMER FOR A MINIMUM OF 5 MINUTES AND GO THERE!
- [ ] MEDITATION – SET YOUR TIMER FOR A MINIMUM OF 5 MINUTES AND BE PRESENT, IN THE NOW. BREATHE.
- [ ] EXERCISE – DID YOU MOVE AT LEAST 30 MINUTES TODAY?
- [ ] FUEL – EAT 80% NUTRIENT DENSE FOOD THAT ENERGIZES YOU

I WAS MOST GRATEFUL FOR TODAY

Good Evening Gorgeous!

I LOVE TO GIVE. TODAY I GAVE

CHEERS TO ME!!!
LET'S CELEBRATE MY SUCCESSES FOR THE DAY

TODAY **is the best day** **EVER !!!**

DATE:

NOTES
- -
- -
- -

1. -
2. -
3. -

my top 3 goals for today that will lead me to joy !!

6AM – 9AM

10AM – 1PM

2PM – 5PM

6PM – 9PM

10PM – 6AM

make sure you get your sleep!

I AM BRILLIANT
gorgeous
TALENTED AND FABULOUS

GOOD MORNING *gorgeous!*

I AM GRATEFUL FOR

MY MANTRA *for today!*

FUN!!! TODAY FOR FUN I WILL

- [ ] VISUALIZATION – SET YOUR TIMER FOR A MINIMUM OF 5 MINUTES AND GO THERE!
- [ ] MEDITATION – SET YOUR TIMER FOR A MINIMUM OF 5 MINUTES AND BE PRESENT, IN THE NOW, BREATHE.
- [ ] EXERCISE – DID YOU MOVE AT LEAST 30 MINUTES TODAY?
- [ ] FUEL – EAT 80% NUTRIENT DENSE FOOD THAT ENERGIZES YOU

I WAS MOST GRATEFUL FOR TODAY

Good Evening Gorgeous!

I LOVE TO GIVE. TODAY I GAVE

CHEERS TO ME!!!
LET'S CELEBRATE MY SUCCESSES FOR THE DAY

TODAY

is the best day

EVER !!!

DATE:

NOTES ---------------------------

----

1. --------------------------
2. --------------------------
3. --------------------------

my top 3 goals for today that will lead me to joy !!

6AM – 9AM

10AM – 1PM

2PM – 5PM

6PM – 9PM

10PM – 6AM

make sure you get your sleep!

I AM BRILLIANT
gorgeous
TALENTED AND FABULOUS

GOOD MORNING gorgeous!

I AM GRATEFUL FOR

MY MANTRA *for today!*

FUN!!! TODAY FOR FUN I WILL

- VISUALIZATION – SET YOUR TIMER FOR A MINIMUM OF 5 MINUTES AND GO THERE!
- MEDITATION – SET YOUR TIMER FOR A MINIMUM OF 5 MINUTES AND BE PRESENT, IN THE NOW. BREATHE.
- EXERCISE – DID YOU MOVE AT LEAST 30 MINUTES TODAY?
- FUEL – EAT 80% NUTRIENT DENSE FOOD THAT ENERGIZES YOU

I WAS MOST GRATEFUL FOR TODAY

Good Evening Gorgeous!

I LOVE TO GIVE. TODAY I GAVE

CHEERS TO ME!!!
LET'S CELEBRATE MY SUCCESSES FOR THE DAY

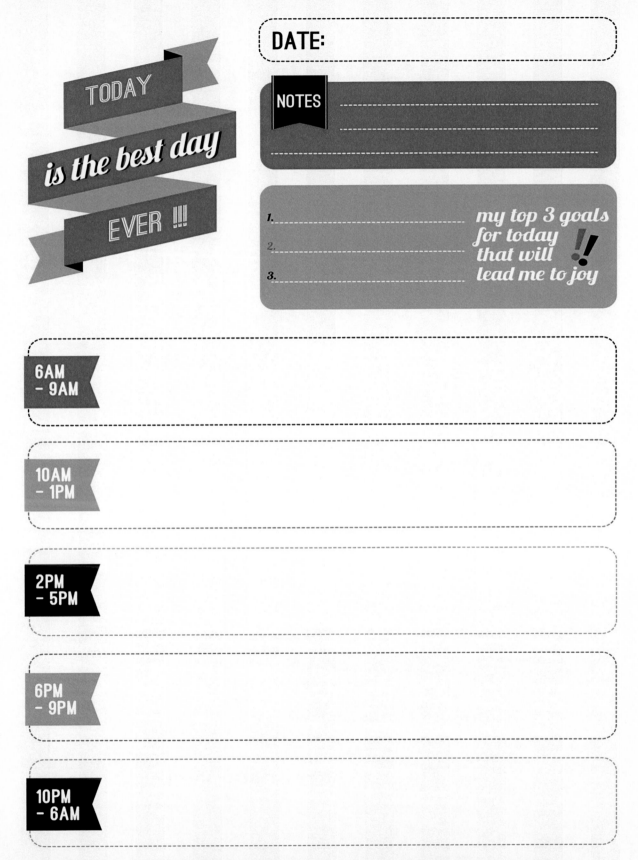

TODAY is the best day EVER !!!

DATE:

NOTES

----

1. -------------------------
2. -------------------------
3. -------------------------

my top 3 goals for today that will lead me to joy !!

6AM – 9AM

10AM – 1PM

2PM – 5PM

6PM – 9PM

10PM – 6AM

make sure you get your sleep!

I AM BRILLIANT
gorgeous
TALENTED AND FABULOUS

GOOD MORNING
gorgeous!

I AM GRATEFUL FOR

MY MANTRA

for today!

FUN!!! TODAY FOR FUN I WILL

☐ VISUALIZATION – SET YOUR TIMER FOR A MINIMUM OF 5 MINUTES AND GO THERE!

☐ MEDITATION – SET YOUR TIMER FOR A MINIMUM OF 5 MINUTES AND BE PRESENT, IN THE NOW. BREATHE.

☐ EXERCISE – DID YOU MOVE AT LEAST 30 MINUTES TODAY?

☐ FUEL – EAT 80% NUTRIENT DENSE FOOD THAT ENERGIZES YOU

I WAS MOST GRATEFUL FOR TODAY

Good Evening Gorgeous!

I LOVE TO GIVE.
TODAY I GAVE

CHEERS TO ME!!!
LET'S CELEBRATE MY SUCCESSES FOR THE DAY

TODAY
is the best day
EVER !!!

DATE:

NOTES

----

1. --
2. --
3. --

*my top 3 goals
for today
that will !!
lead me to joy*

6AM – 9AM

10AM – 1PM

2PM – 5PM

6PM – 9PM

10PM – 6AM

make sure you get your sleep!

I AM BRILLIANT
gorgeous
TALENTED AND FABULOUS

GOOD MORNING *gorgeous!*

I AM GRATEFUL FOR

....

....

....

MY MANTRA

for today!

....

....

....

FUN!!! TODAY FOR FUN I WILL

....

....

....

- ☐ VISUALIZATION – SET YOUR TIMER FOR A MINIMUM OF 5 MINUTES AND GO THERE!
- ☐ MEDITATION – SET YOUR TIMER FOR A MINIMUM OF 5 MINUTES AND BE PRESENT, IN THE NOW. BREATHE.
- ☐ EXERCISE – DID YOU MOVE AT LEAST 30 MINUTES TODAY?
- ☐ FUEL – EAT 80% NUTRIENT DENSE FOOD THAT ENERGIZES YOU

I WAS MOST GRATEFUL FOR TODAY

....

....

....

....

....

....

Good Evening Gorgeous!

I LOVE TO GIVE. TODAY I GAVE

....

....

....

CHEERS TO ME!!!
LET'S CELEBRATE MY SUCCESSES FOR THE DAY

....

....

....

....

TODAY *is the best day* **EVER !!!**

DATE:

NOTES

my top 3 goals for today that will lead me to joy

1.
2.
3.

6AM – 9AM

10AM – 1PM

2PM – 5PM

6PM – 9PM

10PM – 6AM

make sure you get your sleep!

I AM BRILLIANT
gorgeous
TALENTED AND FABULOUS

GOOD MORNING *gorgeous!*

I AM GRATEFUL FOR

MY MANTRA

for today!

FUN!!! TODAY FOR FUN I WILL

☐ VISUALIZATION – SET YOUR TIMER FOR A MINIMUM OF 5 MINUTES AND GO THERE!

☐ MEDITATION – SET YOUR TIMER FOR A MINIMUM OF 5 MINUTES AND BE PRESENT, IN THE NOW. BREATHE.

☐ EXERCISE – DID YOU MOVE AT LEAST 30 MINUTES TODAY?

☐ FUEL – EAT 80% NUTRIENT DENSE FOOD THAT ENERGIZES YOU

I WAS MOST GRATEFUL FOR TODAY

Good Evening Gorgeous!

I LOVE TO GIVE. TODAY I GAVE

CHEERS TO ME!!!
LET'S CELEBRATE MY SUCCESSES FOR THE DAY

TODAY

is the best day

EVER !!!

DATE:

NOTES --

----

1. ---------------------------------------
2. ---------------------------------------
3. ---------------------------------------

my top 3 goals for today that will lead me to joy !!

6AM – 9AM

10AM – 1PM

2PM – 5PM

6PM – 9PM

10PM – 6AM

make sure you get your sleep!

I AM BRILLIANT
gorgeous
TALENTED AND FABULOUS

GOOD MORNING *gorgeous!*

I AM GRATEFUL FOR

MY MANTRA

for today!

FUN!!! TODAY FOR FUN I WILL

- [ ] VISUALIZATION – SET YOUR TIMER FOR A MINIMUM OF 5 MINUTES AND GO THERE!
- [ ] MEDITATION – SET YOUR TIMER FOR A MINIMUM OF 5 MINUTES AND BE PRESENT, IN THE NOW. BREATHE.
- [ ] EXERCISE – DID YOU MOVE AT LEAST 30 MINUTES TODAY?
- [ ] FUEL – EAT 80% NUTRIENT DENSE FOOD THAT ENERGIZES YOU

I WAS MOST GRATEFUL FOR TODAY

Good Evening Gorgeous!

I LOVE TO GIVE. TODAY I GAVE

CHEERS TO ME!!!
LET'S CELEBRATE MY SUCCESSES FOR THE DAY

TODAY is the best day EVER !!!

DATE:

NOTES

1.
2.
3.

my top 3 goals for today that will lead me to joy !!

6AM – 9AM

10AM – 1PM

2PM – 5PM

6PM – 9PM

10PM – 6AM

make sure you get your sleep!

I AM BRILLIANT
gorgeous
TALENTED AND FABULOUS

GOOD MORNING
gorgeous!

I AM GRATEFUL FOR

- -

- -

- -

MY MANTRA

for today!

- -

- -

- -

- -

FUN!!! TODAY FOR FUN I WILL

- -

- -

- -

☐ VISUALIZATION – SET YOUR TIMER FOR A MINIMUM OF 5 MINUTES AND GO THERE!

☐ MEDITATION – SET YOUR TIMER FOR A MINIMUM OF 5 MINUTES AND BE PRESENT, IN THE NOW. BREATHE.

☐ EXERCISE – DID YOU MOVE AT LEAST 30 MINUTES TODAY?

☐ FUEL – EAT 80% NUTRIENT DENSE FOOD THAT ENERGIZES YOU

I WAS MOST GRATEFUL FOR TODAY

- -

- -

- -

- -

- -

- -

Good Evening Gorgeous!

I LOVE TO GIVE.
TODAY I GAVE

- -

- -

- -

CHEERS TO ME!!!
LET'S CELEBRATE MY SUCCESSES FOR THE DAY

- -

- -

- -

- -

TODAY

is the best day

EVER !!!

DATE:

NOTES

1.
2.
3.

*my top 3 goals
for today
that will
lead me to joy*

6AM
– 9AM

10AM
– 1PM

2PM
– 5PM

6PM
– 9PM

10PM
– 6AM

make sure you get your sleep!

I AM BRILLIANT
gorgeous
TALENTED AND FABULOUS

GOOD MORNING *gorgeous!*

I AM GRATEFUL FOR

MY MANTRA

for today!

FUN!!! TODAY FOR FUN I WILL

- ☐ VISUALIZATION – SET YOUR TIMER FOR A MINIMUM OF 5 MINUTES AND GO THERE!
- ☐ MEDITATION – SET YOUR TIMER FOR A MINIMUM OF 5 MINUTES AND BE PRESENT, IN THE NOW. BREATHE.
- ☐ EXERCISE – DID YOU MOVE AT LEAST 30 MINUTES TODAY?
- ☐ FUEL – EAT 80% NUTRIENT DENSE FOOD THAT ENERGIZES YOU

I WAS MOST GRATEFUL FOR TODAY

Good Evening Gorgeous!

I LOVE TO GIVE. TODAY I GAVE

CHEERS TO ME!!!
LET'S CELEBRATE MY SUCCESSES FOR THE DAY

DATE:

NOTES

----

1. ---------------------------------
2. ---------------------------------
3. ---------------------------------

my top 3 goals for today that will lead me to joy

6AM – 9AM

10AM – 1PM

2PM – 5PM

6PM – 9PM

10PM – 6AM

make sure you get your sleep!

I AM BRILLIANT
gorgeous
TALENTED AND FABULOUS

GOOD MORNING *gorgeous!*

I AM GRATEFUL FOR

MY MANTRA

for today!

FUN!!! TODAY FOR FUN I WILL

☐ VISUALIZATION – SET YOUR TIMER FOR A MINIMUM OF 5 MINUTES AND GO THERE!

☐ MEDITATION – SET YOUR TIMER FOR A MINIMUM OF 5 MINUTES AND BE PRESENT, IN THE NOW. BREATHE.

☐ EXERCISE – DID YOU MOVE AT LEAST 30 MINUTES TODAY?

☐ FUEL – EAT 80% NUTRIENT DENSE FOOD THAT ENERGIZES YOU

I WAS MOST GRATEFUL FOR TODAY

Good Evening Gorgeous!

I LOVE TO GIVE. TODAY I GAVE

CHEERS TO ME!!!
LET'S CELEBRATE MY SUCCESSES FOR THE DAY

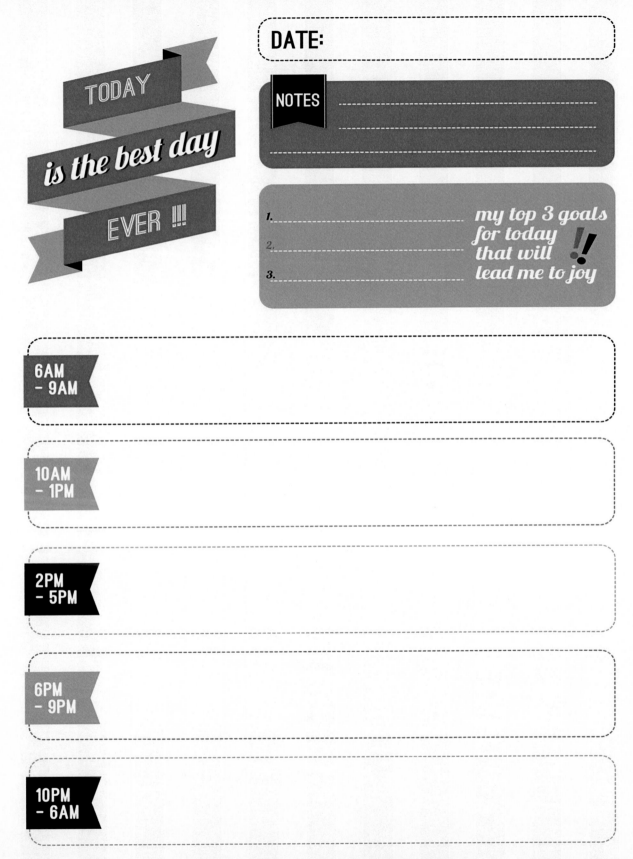

TODAY
is the best day
EVER !!!

DATE:

NOTES

1.
2.
3.

*my top 3 goals
for today
that will
lead me to joy*

6AM
– 9AM

10AM
– 1PM

2PM
– 5PM

6PM
– 9PM

10PM
– 6AM

make sure you get your sleep!

I AM BRILLIANT
gorgeous
TALENTED AND FABULOUS

GOOD MORNING
gorgeous!

I AM GRATEFUL FOR

....
....
....

MY MANTRA

for today!

....
....
....
....

FUN!!! TODAY FOR FUN I WILL

....
....
....

☐ VISUALIZATION – SET YOUR TIMER FOR A MINIMUM OF 5 MINUTES AND GO THERE!

☐ MEDITATION – SET YOUR TIMER FOR A MINIMUM OF 5 MINUTES AND BE PRESENT, IN THE NOW, BREATHE.

☐ EXERCISE – DID YOU MOVE AT LEAST 30 MINUTES TODAY?

☐ FUEL – EAT 80% NUTRIENT DENSE FOOD THAT ENERGIZES YOU

I WAS MOST GRATEFUL FOR TODAY

....
....
....
....
....
....

Good Evening Gorgeous!

I LOVE TO GIVE.
TODAY I GAVE

....
....

CHEERS TO ME!!!
LET'S CELEBRATE MY SUCCESSES FOR THE DAY

....
....
....
....

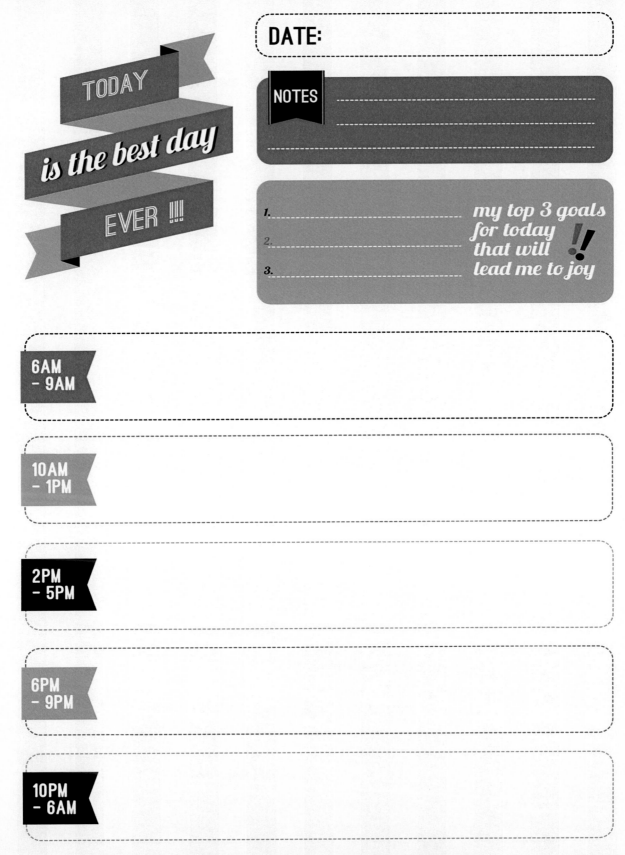

TODAY

is the best day

EVER !!!

DATE:

NOTES

1.
2.
3.

*my top 3 goals
for today
that will
lead me to joy*

6AM – 9AM

10AM – 1PM

2PM – 5PM

6PM – 9PM

10PM – 6AM

make sure you get your sleep!

I AM BRILLIANT
gorgeous
TALENTED AND FABULOUS

GOOD MORNING *gorgeous!*

I AM GRATEFUL FOR

MY MANTRA *for today!*

FUN!!! TODAY FOR FUN I WILL

- ☐ VISUALIZATION – SET YOUR TIMER FOR A MINIMUM OF 5 MINUTES AND GO THERE!
- ☐ MEDITATION – SET YOUR TIMER FOR A MINIMUM OF 5 MINUTES AND BE PRESENT, IN THE NOW. BREATHE.
- ☐ EXERCISE – DID YOU MOVE AT LEAST 30 MINUTES TODAY?
- ☐ FUEL – EAT 80% NUTRIENT DENSE FOOD THAT ENERGIZES YOU

I WAS MOST GRATEFUL FOR TODAY

Good Evening Gorgeous!

I LOVE TO GIVE. TODAY I GAVE

CHEERS TO ME!!!
LET'S CELEBRATE MY SUCCESSES FOR THE DAY

DATE:

TODAY *is the best day* **EVER !!!!**

NOTES --

1. --
2. --
3. --

my top 3 goals for today that will lead me to joy !!

6AM – 9AM

10AM – 1PM

2PM – 5PM

6PM – 9PM

10PM – 6AM

make sure you get your sleep!

I AM BRILLIANT
gorgeous
TALENTED AND FABULOUS

GOOD MORNING
gorgeous!

I AM GRATEFUL FOR

MY MANTRA

for today!

FUN!!! TODAY FOR FUN I WILL

☐ VISUALIZATION – SET YOUR TIMER FOR A MINIMUM OF 5 MINUTES AND GO THERE!

☐ MEDITATION – SET YOUR TIMER FOR A MINIMUM OF 5 MINUTES AND BE PRESENT, IN THE NOW. BREATHE.

☐ EXERCISE – DID YOU MOVE AT LEAST 30 MINUTES TODAY?

☐ FUEL – EAT 80% NUTRIENT DENSE FOOD THAT ENERGIZES YOU

Good Evening Gorgeous!

I WAS MOST GRATEFUL FOR TODAY

I LOVE TO GIVE. TODAY I GAVE

CHEERS TO ME!!!
LET'S CELEBRATE MY SUCCESSES FOR THE DAY

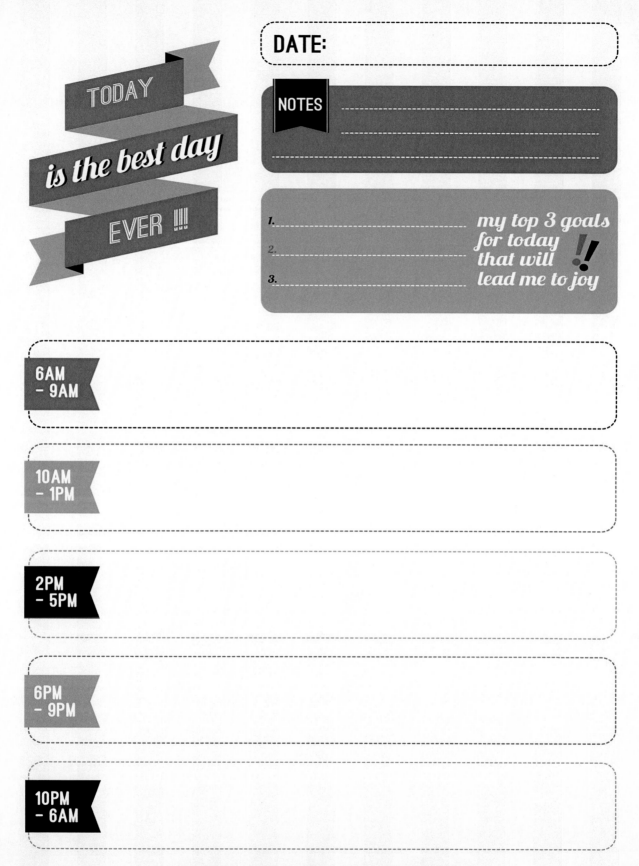

TODAY
is the best day
EVER !!!!

DATE:

NOTES

----

1. ---
2. ---
3. ---

my top 3 goals
for today
that will
lead me to joy

6AM – 9AM

10AM – 1PM

2PM – 5PM

6PM – 9PM

10PM – 6AM

*make sure you get your sleep!

Made in the USA
San Bernardino, CA
22 June 2016